Jewish Identity and the JDL

Jewish Identity and the JDL

by Janet L. Dolgin

Princeton University Press

Princeton, New Jersey

1977

Published by Princeton University Press, Princeton, New Jersey
In the United Kingdom: Princeton University Press, Guildford, Surrey

Library of Congress Cataloging in Publication Data will
be found on the last printed page of this book
Publication of this book has been
aided by The Andrew W. Mellon
Foundation
This book has been composed in Linotype Baskerville

Printed in the United States of America
by Princeton University Press, Princeton, New Jersey

To my parents,
JOSEPH DOLGIN AND BARBARA L. DOLGIN

Table of Contents

Preface

Motionless Dance: "Basic Attitudes"

*Rabbi Menahem Mendel of Vorki was asked what
constitutes a true Jew. He said: "Three things are fitting
for us: upright kneeling, silent screaming, motionless
dance."*

Buber, *Tales of the Hasidim*

THE motionless dance Rabbi Menahem Mendel of Vorki
included as part of the constitution of the "true Jew" con-
trasts with, and yet underscores, the motionless dance that
concerns this study: the first refers to the defensive posture
of the Jew in the encysted ghettos of Eastern Europe; the
second, to a process of absorption of a group of activist Jews
in the United States under conditions of apparent assimilation. These activist Jews, the people of the Jewish Defense
League, first came together in New York City in 1968.
Explicitly denying the reality and viability of assimilation
and of the "melting pot," the JDL resembled a number of
other ethnic-activist movements that developed in the 1960s
and early 1970s.

The subject of this book is something more and something less than the Jewish Defense League. While I have not
written the specific history of the creation and the decline
of JDL, I have examined the processes through which
JDLers constituted their identity within a multi-ethnic
context, and the ideological forms underlying JDLers'
cultural construction of the "Jew" and of the "Other."
Ideology, as used in this book, does not mean merely a set of
beliefs about political or other activities, nor propaganda,
but means rather, following Steve Barnett and Louis Du-

mont, the forms in which reality itself is grounded; ideological forms do not tend to be perceived as such, do not tend to be seen as being there at all; rather, they are taken as "natural," supporting the inevitable. While rejecting the goals of assimilation in America, while forging an image based on Biblical and ancient Jewish symbolisms, JDLers, in fact, used American ideological forms. This combination was part and parcel of the dialectic of absorption identified by Herbert Marcuse, a dialectic in whose terms JDL was at first empowered and later contained and limited. The image of the motionless dance aptly characterizes this process.

This book, adapted from a doctoral dissertation presented to the Department of Anthropology, Princeton University, is based on fourteen months of fieldwork with the Jewish Defense League. During the twelve months between July 1971 and June 1972, I undertook research in New York City; in July and August 1972, I lived at JDL's school in Jerusalem, where a group of about twenty young JDLers were attending a summer leadership training program. In New York I resided in the Boro Park section of Brooklyn, a neighborhood not typical of the NYC areas where Jews reside, but perhaps prototypical of the city's Orthodox Jewish communities. During the period of my fieldwork, JDL's main office, its "Identity Center," was located in the northwestern section of Boro Park. With a population of 84,000, Boro Park is "predominantly Jewish" (Tauber and Kaplan 1968:526), housing upwards of two hundred synagogues, the large majority of which are Orthodox, and approximately thirty all-day Hebrew schools.

I am grateful to the Center for Urban Ethnography for the research grant (No. 17216) that supported this investigation of the JDL, and to the National Endowment for the Humanities for funding the post-doctoral year I used to begin revising my dissertation.

Without Steve Barnett, Leon Fink, and Judith Goldstein, this study would have been infinitely less fascinating for me—and maybe even a little less difficult! Each has been friend and mentor. Steve Barnett stimulated much of the thinking in this book through his inspirational teaching and his own work on South Indian caste, providing a model against which to view Western stratification. I gained considerable insight from the critical readings of, or less formal but equally useful dialogue with, Vincent Crapanzano, Daniel Dolgin, Stephen Dolgin, Lawrence Fisher, David Kemnitzer, John Kirkpatrick, Mark Leone, Alfonso Ortiz, David Schneider, Peter Seitel, Martin Silverman, and Kay Warren. I am especially grateful to JoAnn Magdoff and Richard Parmentier, each of whom read several drafts of this book, and whose suggestions have been incorporated throughout. I am additionally indebted to the works of Louis Dumont, Henri Lefebvre, Herbert Marcuse, Jean-Paul Sartre, and David Schneider.

I want to thank Meir Kahane for allowing me to undertake the research at a time when the Jewish Defense League could easily have perceived my study as an unwanted invasion, Peter Friedman for having shared his own research data with me, and Daniel Dolgin and Nathan Fox for assistance in data collection.

Given the continuing legal and political entanglements of members of the Jewish Defense League and others who helped me with my research, I am obliged to protect their confidences in respecting their civil rights. Therefore, at several points I have had to limit material to that which has already been made available to the public.

Jewish Identity and the JDL

Introduction

AFTER Rome's destruction of the second Temple, the Jews were scattered into the diaspora. In Europe and Russia, the Jews protected themselves against the next expulsion, the next pogrom, in the defending sanctity of ghetto faith. Jewish emancipations came with the Enlightenment in Western Europe during the nineteenth century; paths emerged from the ghettos; the despised defamers of Christ became a "race." Not severed from society any longer by the rituals of a strange, infidelic religion, the Jews of Western Europe were allowed to enter society but were marked as biologically separate, precipitating a situation no less precarious for Jews than that following their earlier heresy, for, as Hannah Arendt writes:

> As far as the Jews were concerned, the transformation of the "crime" of Judaism into the fashionable "vice" of Jewishness was dangerous in the extreme. Jews had been able to escape from Judaism into conversion; from Jewishness there was no escape. A crime, moreover, is met with punishment; a vice can only be exterminated (Arendt 1958:87).

The American Jews came—first the Sephardim of Spain and Portugal by way of Brazil, then the German Jews, and then the Jews of Eastern Europe and Russia, escaping pogroms of the late nineteenth and early twentieth centuries. Here the Jew was an immigrant, but there was a difference: to be an immigrant was said to be normal. There were periods of hardship; that too was normal. To be a Jew no longer meant to be viewed as either moneylender or social recluse. Even the anti-Semitism of the 1920s and 1930s passed with the advent of World War II, as Father Coughlin, the Silver Shirts, the Christian Front, and the *Protocols of the Elders of Zion* were stilled. The exterminators of the Jews of Europe—though that lot resounds through the limits of Jewish time—were felled. In the new State of Israel the American Jew posited a pride, a link, a reaffirmation, and then Zionism also faded into the successes of the 1950s when the Jew was "Jewish," but no one quite knew why: being Jewish, it was suggested, had become a matter of choice. Jews did remain in the early immigration centers of the cities, but most American Jews could finally erase the fears previously incurred through grim historic analogies; they barely remembered what these analogies were.

Other fears came in the 1960s: the fears of being an American. The question of to be or not to be a Jew, of how and when to be a Jew, seemed to pall during the process of seeing what it meant to be an American in the decade of the civil-rights struggle and of cruel "commitments" to war in Vietnam. By the end of that decade, when JDL was conceived, two domains of revitalization among Jews—one international, the other local—were affecting alterations in the cultural construction of Jewishness. The viability of the liberalisms attributed to the American Jews was called into question as the Jews were told in less and less uncertain terms that, at best, their participation in the black power struggle was misguided, as identifications based on race, ethnicity, and sex became more and more explicit, and as the United States' force in Vietnam raged unabated. Then in 1967, consequent to the Six-day War, the beginnings of these shifts combined with the intensifications of Jewishness in America. In the weeks preceding the war, the mighty yet silent nations of the world and, in the weeks after the war, the now vociferous and adamant nations in the United Nations agreed only on the issue of Israel's guilt, harshly suggesting that Israel was not, indeed, a state like other states. But Israel's victory in 1967 offered alternatives to the American Jew who was reminded in the weeks of May and

June of the fears, the insecurities, the old and ever-present weakness of the diaspora Jew. Contributions to Israel rose four-fold over the previous year, more American Jews began to emigrate to Israel than ever before (almost 10,000 in 1970), and a plethora of Jewish student movements, newspapers, and communal fellowships materialized (Glazer 1972). With increasing visibility the young Jew in particular, the dream of the American diaspora, seemed to be affirming unaccustomed modes of being Jewish.

In the years just before the Six-day War, changes of a related sort, though little noticed by the majority of American Jews, had begun to occur within the Orthodox community of New York City, a community of Jews who had been deemed an immigrant vestige. Of the estimated six million American Jews about one tenth are Orthodox, sending their children to *yeshivot* (religious schools), maintaining *kashrut* (dietary laws) in their homes, observing *shabbot* (the sabbath), and in general living according to the laws of traditional Judaism. In the mid-1960s Orthodox American Jewry became increasingly concerned with and involved in American society but, unlike previous examples of Jewish "Americanization," these Jews were reacting in the name of Orthodox Jewry. Religious identification was maintained *through* an "ethnic" insistence; militant response against the "liberalism" of "establishment" Jewry, even against the "liberals" within the Orthodox community itself, focused around issues such as state aid to parochial schools, legislation affecting methods for animal slaughter (an animal is *kosher* only if slaughtered according to specified procedures), and alleviation of the hardships of Soviet Jewry. Politically, Orthodox Jewry began to underscore a commitment to conservative policies and candidates, increasingly solidifying acknowledgments of a political "polarization" within American Jewry. "In the area of political life," wrote Marvin Schick in early 1967, "orthodox Jewry is now evolving into an ethnic pressure group, much the same in character as other ethnic groups whose style and demands have been deprecated by orthodox and non-orthodox Jews alike" (1967:36).

In short, if the question, "Who is the American Jew?" is being raised with new intensity, it is as confounded as ever. The very intensity of the inquiry seems only to make the struggle for an answer more complex. Some Jews share a religion, others a culture, an ethnic identification, a "moral" sense, but Jews are bounded by none of these and can reject them all while remaining "Jewish." Indeed, Glazer and Moynihan (1970) suggest that the negative definition offered by American Jewish fundraising groups is as adequate as any: Who is not the American Jew? And it is significant to note that, in this context, *not* being an American Jew is taken to mean having converted to another religion.

Jewish and non-Jewish perceptions of the Jew have shifted through the ages, and with these shifts Jewish conceptions of past Jewish lifeways have been reconstructed. Some particular legends and aphorisms have served a multiplicity of Jewish communities, tying the Jews of distant cities and divergent beliefs to the sense of a connected past, projecting them into a shared, if uncertain, future. The mere fact that Moses and Abraham, Judith and Bar-Kochba, are known to be and to have been known to other Jews works toward a naturalization of people's Jewish commonality. Historic identification encompasses, even dictates, the faded memories as well as those preserved.

American sociology has tended in recent years to designate "Jews" as one of several American ethnic groups. Shibutani and Kwan's *Ethnic Stratification* (1965) defines an ethnic group as a people who see themselves and are seen by others as "being alike" on the basis of a "common ancestry"; Jews are used as an illustrative case. Among the designations that have been applied to the Jews through history—a race, a nation, a religion, a culture—"ethnicity" seems now to be the stressed characterization in the United States. Social scientists have statistically described value patterns that are Jewish and have analyzed stereotypes attributed to the Jew (generally by the anti-Semite), but their accuracy is called into question in light of the Jewish Defense League or, perhaps the Jewish Defense League seems anomalous in light of these values. For example, drawing from Nathan Glazer's depiction of the American Jew, Milton Gordon writes: "The Jews arrived in America with the middle-class values of thrift, sobriety, ambition, desire for education, ability to postpone immediate gratification for the sake of long-range goals, and aversion to violence already internalized" (1964:186). This description is echoed by Shibutani and Kwan in their presentation of the results of the New Haven study by Fred L. Strodtbeck and others comparing Italian and Jewish social mobility. In particular, "Among Jews a wealthy man without some learning is regarded as vulgar. Most Jews are unimpressed by physical prowess, but an Italian manual worker never has to be ashamed of his strength" (Shibutani and Kwan 1965:65). Where do these observations lead when considering the Jews of JDL, who are as self-consciously Jewish as they are militant, and who are not, to say the least, ashamed of their physical strength? The one thing almost nobody would have predicted in the 1950s was a "Jewish defense league"—certainly not in a country where Jews have been successful and where anti-Semitism has seemed at least as unpopular as it has anywhere in the history of the second diaspora. Is JDL the exception that proves the rule? Are the league's militance and pride in physical defense an aberration in an otherwise consistent group of people? Is JDL unJewish, and if so, statistically, or in some more profound sense? And what, furthermore, *is* the relation between beliefs in "common ancestry" and "value patterns" imputed to the ancestors' common descendants? Although answers proliferate—from American sociology, from major American Jewish groups, *and* from the Jewish Defense League—there is a surprising dearth of analysis as to what people really do mean when they assert common ancestry.

This book is about a group of people—the people of the Jewish Defense League—who assert a common ancestry and who think, moreover, that it is a common ancestry encompassing those Jews who "value" learning and abhor violence. Common ancestry can be refurbished or re-instituted; it can be re-defined or set aside, and it certainly has as much to do with the present as with the past. Knowing the fact of "common ancestry" is knowing very little. The symbols through which JDL established *its* common ancestry ("with all Jews") were not taken from obscure mythology or archaic testimonials. Abraham? Moses? Judah Maccabee? Massada? The Warsaw ghetto resistors? Even "never again," the motto of the Jewish Defense League, and the star of David with a fist planted in its center—for what Jew no matter how pacific would not condone resistance to the Nazi terror? Hardly the stuff for refutation. Or is it? The same Moses who received the Ten Commandments from God and (as someone once said) established the Jewish nation and the roots of Western civilization in one interaction, can also be posed as the man who did not "form a committee to study the grass-roots of Egyptian anti-Semitism" when he saw an Egyptian striking a Jew; "He smote the Egyptian and buried him in the sand" (Exodus 2:11). And the same Massada, praised and mourned as the sign of the last Jew in second century Palestine, can also be posed as a fortress of violence whose call to the contemporary Jew is "bury your life-ways before they bury you."

JDL has offered American Jewry some new slogans and some twists to received "scripture." It has variously been seen as the agent because of which, or despite which, the Soviet Union began to let increased numbers of Jews emigrate to Israel in the early 1970s. It has been described as "the flea which moved the elephant, Russia" and as a minor nuisance. One New York City official said the biggest effect

JDL had on the city was to "cause an extra lay-out of money to surround the Soviet Mission with police." It has been labeled "the end of American Jewry" in both a negative sense ("if we can produce this, we might as well give up") and a positive sense ("we in JDL let the Jew here in America see that his only place is in Israel"). It has caused journalists to ponder: "JDL: heroes or hooligans?" and Israelis to mutter, "*We* need *their* defense?"

What JDL offers the anthropologist is a chance to look at a group of people who are calling into question the meanings of self, religion, nationality, and of their own place in the scheme of things. Values and beliefs that had almost come to be thought of as somehow "naturally" representing the American Jew are questioned by the mere existence of JDL. JDLers have deliberately fashioned a stance toward being "Jewish" and have unabashedly projected that stance as the proper perspective, the "authentic" perspective, of all American Jews, indeed of all Jews. JDL's pronouncements have been met with scorn and opposition, with disavowals and condemnations, from a large proportion of American Jews who, through the focus of their conflicts with JDL, have framed and articulated their own conceptions of what it means and what it should mean to be a Jew in America. JDL compels the anthropologist to work not because its members agree that Jews have a common ancestry but because it has consciously defined (and defended) unexpected notions of what a Jew should be and do, notions that, once generated, have propelled JDLers and other Jews to reconsider the essence and the uses of "Jewish" common ancestry in relation to themselves and to non-Jews.

CHAPTER I

The Activities of the Jewish Defense League

IN February 1973 a swastika was painted on the door of a house in Queens, New York. Those responsible were not identified, but the intentions of the "artists" (a word used by the owner of the house) were clearly threatening. A man claiming to represent the Hebrew Defense Association (HDA) arrived to offer his movement's "solution" for the family's "problem." Family members, already frightened and anxious, disputed the morality and viability of the militant reaction suggested by the HDAer. Some took sides against the HDA, characterizing the association as "strong-arm" and "vigilante"; the father of the family, however, found the HDAer's stance to exemplify "straight-thinking."

This scenario, serious though it was, included an element of humor, a humor that played off the rather unexpected fact that, with the exception of the HDAer, none of the participants were Jews. Events turned toward tragedy; the HDAer was the victim of a murder: *this* was seen as peculiar.

The episode just related formed one plot of "All in the Family," a television situation-comedy produced by CBS; the door on which the swastika appeared was a prop in a play; the protagonist approving HDA tactics was Archie Bunker; and the HDAer was an actor, who, it might be noted, appears as a Puerto Rican on the serial "Sanford and Son."[1]

" 'For too long,' he [Rabbi Meir Kahane] said, 'the Jewish people have been patsies.' He gathered a group of young men about him, and he spoke to them of the extermination of six million Jews in Nazi Germany. 'Never

[1] The episode of "All in the Family" about the Hebrew Defense Association is analyzed by Magdoff and Dolgin n.d.

again,' he said, and it became the group's slogan. He charged that the black residents of Williamsburg and Crown Heights were terrorizing Jewish businessmen and old people; and he sent the young men forth, armed with clubs, to patrol the areas. As the organization grew, it acquired a name, the Jewish Defense League, and a summer camp where members were instructed in judo, karate and the use of firearms. The program expanded: the league entered the political arena, heckling Mayor Lindsay for being too much concerned about blacks and too little about Jews. About six months ago, Rabbi Kahane set the group on a new course, a series of vigils dramatizing the alleged oppression of Jews in the Soviet Union. It brought the Jewish Defense League, and the rabbi from Queens, to the center of the world stage."— *New York Times* (January 17, 1971)

"The Reb's [Rabbi Kahane's] heart was broken when he saw Jews were being beaten up. Every single thing he saw happening to Jews he didn't like. It was really hard to make up an organization. Thank God we got it. . . . Before JDL, I remember once I was walking to work after school. I went to work every day after school. This guy comes up to us and says, 'dirty Jew.' He was carrying rocks and threw them. I was with my brother and sister and one rock hit my sister. And another time I was just walking slowly on the street and four guys were behind me saying, 'Let's kill the Jew.' . . . And then I first heard the Reb speak about helping your brothers. . . . I was about eighteen, and I started to cry. Like he said the word. Help our people. Help our brothers not to be killed. That piece of word broke my heart in pieces, and that's why I came and why I joined the JDL. That was a few years ago."—Twenty-one-year-old male JDLer (November 1971)[2]

[2] The speaker, intensely involved with JDL, was from an extremely Orthodox family. Although born in America. Yiddish was his first language.

The television episode and the two quotations are presented here in reverse order to their actual occurrence: a group of people joined together to form the Jewish Defense League; the league became the focus of public media coverage; and then CBS used a fictionalized JDL in a television show. Although the latter of these two media portraits of JDL was explicitly fabricated, while the former was defined as a reporting of the facts, they alike contributed to the actualization of certain of the notions being suggested (in each characterization) about the league; the appearance of JDL on television as a "Hebrew Defense Association" was a fulfillment of the "Reb" who "said the word" and represented another attaining of "the center of the world stage," referred to by the *New York Times* in 1971: the very fact that "All in the Family" used JDL as the basis of a plot, signals a success for the league.[3] But there is more to it than that: JDLers themselves played with myth and history. For JDLers, the development of their movement became something more than a set of facts pertaining to the time and place in which the league came to be. From the start the Jewish Defense League encapsulated itself as a legend, that legend becoming, of course, another fact. JDLers engaged myth to empower history and used history in verifying myth; JDLers recounted league episodes, and, in the telling, sustained a sense of protest embodied in accounts of

[3] For the most part I use the past tense in writing of JDL's activities for several reasons: although JDL is extant today (1975), the period I am primarily dealing with starts with the league's beginnings in 1968 and continues through September 1972, when my fieldwork ended; aspects of JDL's formal organization, specific membership, and even official ideology, change rapidly. In addition, the time between 1968 and 1972 forms for JDLers themselves an "historic" period; in June 1972 Meir Kahane, JDL's foremost leader, returned to Israel, where he and his family had settled in 1971, and he did not come to the United States again until autumn 1974. When speaking more generally about JDLers' perspectives, their relations to themselves and their world, I sometimes use the present tense.

heroism. Yet the variants (the fictions, the myths, the histories) folded in upon themselves, for increasingly JDLers' own conceptions of their movement were built from communications in the public media. Particularly after the movement expanded to the point where most JDLers no longer participated in each league demonstration or action, television and newspaper reports served as a vital source of information for leaguers about the activities of their group. Exposure on page one of daily newspapers was the evidence of "success."

In speaking about the growth of their movement, JDLers talked of a period of early development (1968-1969): they recast these beginnings in terms of a heroism in the absence of "fame" and public attention—the bravery of the actor not yet observed. Members' accounts of league development after about 1969, on the other hand, emphasize the league actions and episodes that received media attention. Concomitantly, members' tellings of league activities after 1969 are focused through a series of "events," clearly demarcated and linearly organized. The news reports provide a form through which the objectification of JDL's history for league members themselves can be effected. In consequence, a tension develops between the separation of each JDLer from that history and the sense of participation and conscious creation that JDLers have (and believe they should have) vis-à-vis the league. Or, to say it differently, various modes of reification are co-existent: the JDLer, inclined to conceive of the league through one sort of (created) history, is compelled to entertain, and then retain, an entirely different variant. "The very principal of myth," writes Roland Barthes is that "it transforms history into nature. . . . what causes mythical speech to be uttered is perfectly explicit, but it is immediately frozen into something natural; it is not read as motive, but as reason" (1972:129). What Barthes calls "myth" is the essence of reification—the course through which the histories people make are naturalized.

The news (and with it, history) may secure itself around and within the Event:[4] the uniform and the uninterpreted are segmented and selected out in the name of the eventful. Linear time is reified through the seriality of events which are, in turn, taken to be the very products of linear time: historic continuity, that is to say, finds its composition in the linking of discrete episodes that history itself reunites. Thus Lévi-Strauss says: "History seems to restore to us, not separate states, but the passage from one state to another in a continuous form" (1966: 256).

News recedes into history where, apparently risking nothing, it remains for possible classification as "historically significant." And here, risk reemerges with all the equivocality of the original News. "Intonation matters," writes Joseph Levenson in *Confucian China and Its Modern Fate.* "We may describe an item in the human record as historically (really) significant, or as (merely) historically significant" (1968:III, 85). The "historical significance" of the Jewish Defense League almost immediately became an object of debate: while JDLers intone "really," their critics —especially within the New York Jewish community—as frequently intone "merely." One anti-JDL employee of a secular Jewish organization, based in NYC, said: "They [JDL] may be important to history. I don't deny that . . . the trouble is the attention they're now getting." This intonation carries a paradox of another sort: the devaluation implied in "merely" is attenuated in its very formulation, a formulation that judges the present as significant through the imagined eyes of the future.

JDLers and their critics, despite discrepant judgments on the league, tend to agree in their enumerations of the Events of JDL, the Events that made JDL newsworthy, precipitating the "scandal" JDL effected within the New York Jewish community. JDL was a scandal—indeed, JDLers themselves

---

[4] The capitalization of "Events," "News," "Action," "Other," as with several other words throughout, is intended to indicate that the concept at hand has been reified, i.e., is taken as natural.

prize the tag—not through the facts of poverty, religious Orthodoxy, or even Jewish militancy; these existed before and without JDL. Rather, the Events, because they were reported, made it impossible to ignore or overlook JDL. And that was the scandal. Moreover, it was a scandal that, once imagined, could be regenerated and sustained, for as Pierre Vilar suggests, "professional sensationalists like to multiply 'events.' 'Historic facts' are all the rage on a day of lunar landings or barricades" (1973:79).

To understand the cultural construction of JDL, it is necessary to examine the context within which JDL grew and in terms of which JDLers constituted themselves through their movement. JDLers built barricades, and that has been recorded. But the "sensational" episodes in JDL's short history tell only part of the story: there is, in addition, the struggle of JDL to define the essence of Jewish identity and to enact that identity in its own "defense," to create the terms within which to act and the terms in whose name ethnic action could be authenticated. In seeking to base action on ethnicity, JDL has been faced with a series of contradictions. In part the contradictions must be seen in light of the very necessity for JDL to be "newsworthy"; but, inversely, contradictions appear to be absorbed in the league's activities, which have been reified—as Events— through the medium of news; this was possible because history (past news) is definitionally freed of disturbing contradiction.

A dominant contradiction in the Jewish Defense League's project to en*act* ethnicity was present from the first. In a broader frame, this contradiction occurs generally in the United States, where class tends to be denied as a foundation of group identity and action. Even where ethnicity has been admitted and paraded, the publication of class identity remains taboo. Indeed, "ethnicity" replaces and masks class consciousness, and has lain the ground for the particular form that absorption—the appropriation of negation in the name of that which "is"—has taken in the U. S. in the last decade (cf., Marcuse 1964).[5] The process of JDL's development illustrates the dialectic of absorption: the league in large part modeled its presentation of identity on identities presented by other ethnic activist movements, especially black groups (which thus became both model and antagonist for JDL); and, JDL's own slogans and signs of identity were quickly taken up and used by other groups (from non-Jewish activist movements to what JDLers called the "Jewish establishment").

JDL was created in the spring of 1968 by a small group of Orthodox Jews concerned with the explicitly particularistic issues of "crime in the streets," "black anti-Semitism," "liberal do-nothing city government," and "changing neighborhoods." From the start the league's undisputed leader was Meir Kahane, a rabbi who at the time of JDL's founding worked as an associate editor and columnist for the *Jewish Press*, an English-language weekly newspaper published in Brooklyn.[6] As the JDL spread in championing a host of

[5] In U. S. history, for the most part, the self-conscious espousal of "ethnic" (national, religious, racial) identity has been submerged under a Melting Pot ideology, the presumption that all difference should (would) vanish in the name of equality. Ethnic revivals of the 1960s, growing from the civil-rights movement in particular, came to be seen (both positively and negatively) as effective forms of protest. The analysis of JDL, a movement created within the context of this revival, is, finally, the analysis of effective absorption, and not of protest (see chapter 2 for an extended discussion).

[6] Along with Kahane, Bertram Zweibon, a New York City attorney, and Morton Delinsky, who moved to Israel soon after JDL began, were instrumental in the league's creation. Early, JDL printed "biographical data" sheets about Kahane and Zweibon. Kahane, entitled "Executive Director" of JDL, is described as a native of Brooklyn, born August 1, 1932, the father of four children, and holder of "a B.A. from Brooklyn College (54), LLB from the New York Law School (57), M.A. in International Law, New York University (57), and he was ordained as a Rabbi at the Mirrer Yeshiva, Brooklyn, N. Y., in 1957." Kahane is noted to have been director of the Center for Political Studies, "a private research firm in Washington, D. C.," associate editor of the Jewish Press, member in the Brit Trumpeldor movement, and on the

national and international "Jewish concerns," the membership grew to contain a wide spectrum of Jews. JDLers, by
the early 1970s, included wealthy members, young members,
and suburban members. These recruits shared with the
original membership an expressed marginality to Jewish
institutions and groups ordinarily considered as most important in America—groups JDLers called the "Jewish
establishment"[7]—and a sense of personal authenticity as

National Executive Board of B'nai Akiva. The most publicized and
extensive, though rather unfriendly account of Kahane appeared in
the *New York Times* in early 1971. The article's most startling dis-
closure was that for a time during the 1960s Kahane had lived a "dual
existence," writing and working in Washington under the alias Michael
King (Kaufman, 1/24/71). As King, Kahane and Joseph Churba, a
rabbi and professor at the U. S. Air University at Maxwell Air Force
Base in Alabama, had established a research firm seeking government
contracts, and in 1966 had tried to set up what they called the July
Fourth Movement to quell sentiment against U. S. involvement in
Vietnam. The two men wrote and published a book entitled *The
Jewish Stake in Vietnam*, listing Michael King as a third author. Later,
Kahane explained he had used both names so that people who knew
him by either could identify him. Although Kahane, and following him,
other JDLers, called the piece a "hatchet job," denying inferences
drawn from it that he had had CIA contacts or had worked for the
House UnAmerican Activities Committee, the implications of the
Times story rebounded past JDL's explanations, remaining a source of
journalists' queries and a foundation for aspersions against the league.

JDL officially portrays Zweibon, the league's "General Counsel," as a
"long-term advocate of Jewish rights." He holds a B. A. in political
science and an LLB (1954) from New York University. On JDL's
biographic data sheet, Zweibon is said to have been "President of the
Progressive Republican Club, Chancellor of the Knights of Pythias,
and a member of the Board of Directors of the Alumni Association of
the Emanuel Brotherhood at the Midtown YMHA" as well as an
"active" delegate to the National Council of Young Israel.

[7] To JDLers the "Jewish establishment" meant any Jews who allowed their wealth and security to overstep "authentic Jewishness."
Specifically, however, the "Jewish establishment" denoted a set of organizations: B'nai B'rith, founded by German Jews in America in 1845,
of which the Anti-Defamation League (ADL), founded in 1913 and
active in fighting anti-Semitism during the 1920s and 1930s particularly.

Jews. (The opposing definitions of Self—JDLer—as isolated and as central is found throughout JDL's development.) The early JDL members were people who did not see their daily concerns (religious education for their children, fear of crime, economic hardships) tended by city government or reflected in the programs and perspectives of the major secular Jewish organizations (e.g., B'nai B'rith, American Jewish Committee, American Jewish Congress), groups characterized by JDLers as falsely representing the Jewish position to non-Jewish America. The early, blatant expressions of disdain for "establishment Jewry" later provided the form in terms of which JDLers could become the ("natural") guardians of world Jewry. But this came later. The scenario within which thirty JDLers joined together at their first meeting was that of racial and ethnic[8] antagonism: JDL was created *against* the Other.

The league was created by middle-aged, lower- and lower-

---

is a part; the American Jewish Committee (AJC), formed in 1906 by German Jews in the U. S. after early-twentieth-century pogroms in Russia and involved in defense against anti-Semitism; the American Jewish Congress (AJ Cong), which, when established in 1918, provided a forum in opposition to what its early members saw as the wealthier, anti-Zionist, more assimilated Jews of the committee. The Socialist-Zionist and early proponent of the congress, Nachman Syrkin, described Jewish antipathy to the congress's creation in words not far from those a JDLer might have chosen some fifty years later in voicing opposition to the committee and the congress alike: "Jewish Wall Street," Arthur A. Goren reports Syrkin's having said, "does not want this Congress, . . . those men are standing against democracy, and they are not only treacherous to the Jewish people, but to the spirit of America" (1970: 219). The Federation of Jewish Philanthropies, founded in 1917 to coordinate charitable activity within the Jewish community, was a frequent object of JDL's attacks against organized American Jews.

[8] Generally I use the terms race and racial to indicate blacks and whites and ethnic and ethnicity to indicate white American groups basing their identity on "blood" and/or land. At times, however, "ethnic" as in popular usage, indicates both sets of relations; the application of an ethnic model to other groups (e.g., feminism) is part and parcel of absorption.

middle-class Jews, reacting to a situation in which they perceived themselves the forgotten people; not wealthy or powerful in a land where Jews were viewed as both, they also resented "benefits" they felt liberal politicians were bestowing upon blacks and other ethnic groups but from which they were somehow exempted. The people who founded JDL and whose concerns remained preeminent within the movement lived in Williamsburg and Boro Park in Brooklyn and on the Lower East Side in Manhattan. The men drove trucks and taxis, were employed in city offices, owned small businesses, often in neighborhoods once Jewish, now largely black. The women worked as secretaries and clerks; they served as waitresses and salespeople, frequently in their husbands' stores; they had heard of feminism, and their lives had not been totally unaffected by the movement, but most JDL women (with the frequent exception of young women, especially those attending college) accepted a subordinate position as rightfully theirs and within the league did not seriously compete for general leadership positions. Whether through choice or through compulsion, the first league members had remained "Jews,"[9] self-consciously denying assimilation to be a viable alternative. JDLers conclusively encompassed the possibility for the development of class consciousness by that of ethnic consciousness in defining their perceived marginality as an index of authenticity (by, for instance, denying the "Jewishness" of "establishment" Jewish groups); the foundation for identity became increasingly one of substance and thus universal (i.e., for all Jews) and "natural."

The structure within which JDLers defined themselves was fashioned through the dual relations of Jew to non-Jew and of JDL Jew to Jew. White ethnic group identity in the late 1960s was largely elaborated in opposition to perceived threats of the black movement; the perception of these

[9] JDL's culturally constructed meaning of the "Jew" is discussed throughout subsequent chapters.

threats combined familiar racisms with a new fear of being replaced. JDLers did not simply imagine themselves in negative relation to blacks; a conglomerate pattern developed in which the league rejected a set of "liberal" models and institutions (both Jewish and non-Jewish) that were equally the targets of black, and even more of radical, groups. That rejection became the basis for JDL's own "radical" posture that later attracted college students and middle-class Jews, not part of the population among whom JDL gained its first note.

The scenario within which the league came to be is well represented by the New York City teachers' strike of 1968. That strike—actually three strikes between September and mid-November—crystallized from a demonstration project in public school decentralization financed by the Ford Foundation in Ocean Hill-Brownsville, a Brooklyn neighborhood with a largely black population.[10] Decentralization was to provide a framework for local communities to gain decision-making power in educating their children; the Ocean Hill-Brownsville project was designed to give blacks control in a white-dominated school system with a large black student body. From the start there was tension between the Ocean Hill-Brownsville governing board and the United Federation of Teachers (UFT), but the immediate determination of the strike and the matter around which the conflicts arose was a recommendation of the district's governing board in April 1968 to dismiss nineteen personnel, considered in opposition to the experimental project.[11] When Superintend-

[10] For extended analyses and description of the teachers' strike, at the time of its occurrence the source of innumerable journalistic accounts, see, e.g., Epstein 1968; Mayer 1969; Rubinstein 1970; Weisbord and Stein 1970.

[11] Almost all those designated for dismissal from the district were Jews, who comprise a large part of the UFT membership. The UFT proclaimed that the personnel (thirteen teachers, five assistant principals, and one principal) had been summarily fired; proponents of the district's governing board and others maintained that the board had suggested reassignment of these teachers, who were said to be under-

ent of Schools Bernard Donovan called for the return of the dismissed teachers to the district, local parents, acting from years of anger at a school system perceived to be immune to concerns of educating their children, prevented the teachers from entering the schools.[12] The teachers returned in May with police escort; in September, the conflicts no nearer solution, approximately 95% of the city's teachers did not report for work on the first day of the fall term. The original contestation of the experimental project—which had been given, in what was an apparent paradox, institutional support and government sanction—was met with the counter-tactics of the UFT; the tactics of each side turned out to be the same as those of the other. Hesitancies about racist and anti-Semitic expression vanished; discourse was found to allow increased revelation of the codes through which racism had previously been veiled; the dialectic of absorption resulted not only in increased militancy but in a situation where the only allowable definitions of Self and Other became those based in substance—categorizations through "blood" and "land" (cf., Schneider 1968; 1969).

Mediating groups like JDL focused on the terms of conflict, though JDL's actual role in the strike situation was minimal. The league stood for the stabilization of what was; JDL labeled it well: the "defense" of essence. The strike extended a field of activity that, because it was concrete, allowed the Jewish Defense League a real beginning, an extended importance, a name. In particular, JDL responded vigorously to anti-Semitic statements of several black teachers; these teachers illustrated JDL's cry that black anti-Semitism had blossomed and simultaneously offered a model

---

mining the effectiveness of the project. The transfer of teachers and other personnel within the school system had been practiced before the beginnings of community control.

[12] According to Jason Epstein, the Ocean Hill-Brownsville governing board was justified in its apprehension that "the central school administration together with the UFT had decided to sabotage its experiment in community control of the local schools" (1968:31).

for the league's response.[13] Recalling a history of anti-Semitic hiring practices in the U. S., when entrance through the civil service system afforded Jews a chance to attain teaching employment, JDLers saw decentralization as "the beginning of the end." For Jews, said JDLers, decentralization heralded increased hardship by eliminating the government-administered merit system in hiring public employees. JDL spoke explicitly and exclusively for the Jew and thus, almost by definition, consented to the separation of the strike's conflict from itself—from possible definitions of the strike situation not reliant on substance as the only basis of identity and action; at once reductive and generalizing, JDL's analysis characterized the situation as eternal, as inherent in the relations between Jew and non-Jew and thus as essentially static. The particular difficulties facing Jewish teachers were described as another instance of the concerns JDL had identified; the league accused "WASP government" of sacrificing the Jews to protesting blacks; that disposition was called endemic, an instance of the inevitable; in support of their case, JDLers proffered historical analogies and concluded with the assurance that "always, they throw the Jew to the dogs."

Real change, however, is precluded if the patterns inhere in "nature." So JDLers immediately posted their addendum, their rationale: the non-Jew eternally rejected the Jew but the Jew had *become* weak; the Jew had accepted the role of patsy and weakling. JDLers would demonstrate an alternative. Several years later, when JDL became a Zionist movement, the expression of a universal inheritance was given added credence; the combination of "land" (Israel) and "blood" would effectively replace "blood" alone. But in the late 1960s the task was set up as the demonstration of tenacity: the league was tagged vigilante; the tag was only ambivalently denied. And precisely in this demonstration

---

[13] JDLers vociferously supported the UFT against the district governing board, and groups of leaguers escorted teachers past protesting parents into school buildings.

lay JDL's peculiar success—and its failure. The self-conscious creation of a "new Jew" was contained by the league's presentation of conservative politics in forms generally associated with radical protest. JDL declared itself a movement without "politics"—absence of politics being meant to imply the league's universality and relevance for *all Jews*: in the fruition of that projection, the particular concerns of the lower-middle-class Jews who founded JDL were (for the most part unbeknownst to them) dissolved.

An image of JDL was erected, fostered, and generalized by public media interest, which entailed the separation of the league's development from its own context; Jewish "behavior" was endowed with eternal essence and, in the analysis, ultimately disengaged from other referents. A JDL advertisement placed in several newspapers in June 1969 encapsulates the image and its method. The advertisement was headed by a question: "Is This Any Way for Nice Jewish Boys to Behave?" Images of "nice Jewish boys," satirical in almost any context, would seem to have had little to do with JDL, a movement variously characterized as "vigilante," "Jewish Panthers," "Hebrew fighters," and "just plain hoods." JDL imitates in mockery what is already satire.

The advertisement, almost immediately succeeded by a substantial increase in league membership, takes on another significance in light of the subsequent chronicle of JDL development. Within a year the league's attentions had re-focused around the defense of international Jewry, particularly Soviet Jewry; the threats of "hoodlums," "extortionists," "leftists," "rightists," and "do-nothing" government at home receded into the broader concern: "world Jewry." Yet by 1970 and 1971, when the league was the subject of international news coverage for the "militant defense" of Soviet Jewry, JDLers recalled the league's founding in 1968 and its early growth as a bygone era of unheralded stamina and achievement. JDLers, only a few years later, were spinning the legend of their movement as it was "in the days before people heard of us." The six leaguers in sunglasses, pictured in the advertisement of June 1969, represented that legend (for JDLers): the photograph was distributed as a portrait of the myth. When printed, this advertisement was a league commentary on a particular incident, recently transpired. And that incident, not coincidentally, joins in one space the two poles of relations in the present from which JDL's myth was most effectively forged: to "establishment Jewry" and to "black power." The incident in question began as such in early May 1969 with rumors that James Forman, of the National Black Economic Development Conference, was planning to appear at the May 10 Sabbath evening services of Temple Emanu-El, a wealthy Reform temple on Fifth Avenue in Manhattan. Forman, in what was at the least an effective public relations scheme, had made known that he would present his conference's "Manifesto,"—a demand for reparations of $500 million for black suffering in the U. S.—before church and synagogue congregations.[14] Announcing that Jews would not pay for the sins of white America, JDL set out to ensure a defense: Forman would be physically stopped if he came to Emanu-El. The evening of May 10 found a few dozen league members, arrayed with sticks and chains, stationed around the temple's entrance. Forman did not arrive, and in that absence JDL defined a victory; but JDL's presence set off a minor sensation among New York Jewry. The league's "vigilante" performance was resoundingly denounced by representatives of the city's major Jewish organizations. JDL's leadership was aware that the expressions of outrage meant publicity for the league, publicity having been one of the primary aims of the demonstration at Emanu-El in the first place.

In JDL's reaction to the denunciations of the league's activity at Emanu-El, the limitations JDLers imposed on the analysis of their own situation become evident: the "action"

[14] Earlier in the month Forman had put his conference's demands to the Episcopal Church Center and had read the manifesto during Sunday services at Riverside Church in Manhattan.

at Emanu-El stood to oppose and to include the "Jewish establishment." The specificity of JDLers' own conditions (their *real* marginality to the programs of the most powerful Jewish—and non-Jewish—organizations) was announced by JDLers and then blurred in the insistence that they were "acting" for "all Jews"; thus a purposely mythic foundation was extended. JDLers did not doubt the congregants at Emanu-El would disapprove the league's "tactics" there; yet JDLers called their "protection" of Emanu-El a verification of their commitment to "all Jews," who, whether they knew it or not had no immunity to anti-Semitism—as proven, of course, in the "need" for the league's help. "If," grumbled one JDLer about the worshippers at Emanu-El, "they're so dumb they don't see Forman's an anti-Semite, then they're in real trouble." The truths of JDL's delineations were swallowed up in their own exaggeration, in the unrelieved stress on anti-Semitism as the exclusive ground for action—and reaction. A Self ("all Jews"), defined through substance, became increasingly reliant on continued hypostatization of anti-Semitism.

There was however a concrete and crucial difference in the kind of anti-Semitism experienced by JDLers and that acknowledged by middle-class, professional, suburban Jews, who for the most part had been unaffected by direct anti-Semitism since World War II. Furthermore, crime against Jews in the neighborhoods of New York City where poor Jews dwelt, though not primarily the consequence of anti-Semitism, did evoke memories—particularly for those Jews who had emigrated from the small villages of Eastern Europe in the years surrounding World War II—memories from which grew analogies to village pogroms and to the Nazis. "I'm afraid now like I was in Europe," said one elderly JDLer; "God forbid here we face it again." When JDLers saw the funds of Jewish organizations being used to support hospitals and playgrounds or to finance social service programs for non-Jews, the consequences seemed clear: the poor Jew, the religious Jew, was to remain marginal and unprotected.

The list of Events composing JDL's recorded history divides into three domains of activity: early street patrols and protests against anti-Semitism within New York City; an effervescence of JDL fame with the struggle for Soviet Jewry; and then by late 1971 the call for massive *aliyah* (immigration to Israel) of Jews throughout the diaspora. The particular processes of the league's expansion-in-action were not premeditated. JDL's leadership, contending that the Soviet Jewry struggle was always included in the league's general aims, granted that had JDL not attracted scores of young activists in the interim, the militant style of JDL's doings for Soviet Jewry would not have actualized. For others, non-JDLers, the league was a group in search of a cause. "JDL," said one Orthodox New York rabbi, "is like the March of Dimes. Polio's not an issue anymore so they find another cause."

In its first year and a half JDL focused on local, and thus personal, defense; this was direct and unmediated by subsequent ideology. The politics were clear. A non-partisan stance—though never credible—came later. Immediately JDL set up street patrols, deeming city police unable or unwilling to provide protection for inner-city residents.[15] The division between general and particular interests was still transparent: invoking a frontier ideology, physically defending themselves in the name of nothing but that defense, JDLers represented a concretization in extreme form of sentiments shared by many Jews in Boro Park, Williamsburg, Crown Heights, and the Lower East Side. Disagreement in these first months, as later, centered on the tactics, not the reasoning. The notion that Jews for once should

[15] The Maccabees, a small group organized in Crown Heights, Brooklyn, during the late 1960s, provided a precedent for neighborhood Jews attempting to deal directly with street crime. That group, criticized by city government for usurping police functions, had been disbanded (Weisbord and Stein 1970). By the early 1970s, several local synagogue groups, though rejecting JDL, affiliated with the city's auxiliary police program.

defend themselves was, even when rejected in its specificity, received with pride. "I am," said an Orthodox resident of Boro Park, "against them, but I can see why there is pride in them. I wouldn't carry a gun. How can I praise people who carry them?"

Early JDL statements, startling in light of later league ideology, are indicative of an aspect of the process of absorption. A JDL "manifesto," among the league's first official publications, is a good place to view the early formulations. The manifesto, its own form of rhetoric belying the content, is a call for "moderation" in America, a call to the Jew as American. It lacks the Biblical referents and Judaic symbolisms of later league literature: "America has been good to the Jew and the Jew to America." And the manifesto continues:

> And so, as political extremism of Right and Left flourishes; as racism of Black and Backlash light the contemporary skies with frightening colors; as government remains paralyzed and impotent; as too many who should know better cater to and support the madness of extremism, our cities are plunged into chaos, riots ravage whole sections, buildings and establishments are burned and looted, crime drives the innocent into fearful hiding, their homes becoming prisons as the sun goes down. Teachers are driven from their positions by psychotics, demagogues and calculated racist extremists; the democratic fabric begins to rip at the seams; weakness, vacillation and blindness afflict our leaders and the organizations supposedly created to vigorously combat these things. The average American, the average Jew remains frightened, bewildered and lost.[16]

[16] In 1972 one young JDLer, an early member and youth leader, said of the manifesto: "There was stuff in that which could be seen as racist. I once took a survey on how many people had read it, and about 40% had read it, but only 2% understood it."

The use of the political metaphor necessitated a stance toward assimilation, with difference still cast as extremist and thus evil; ethnicity had not quite become the supremely popular form for expressions of self-identity it soon would be. Within two years even the "politics of moderation" could be replaced with ethnic imagery. This shift, from a discourse on politics to one on ethnicity, brought both JDL's outspoken denial of assimilation as a productive posture and the increasing use of forms of action that were pre-eminently absorbable: potential negations of the status quo were thus encompassed by a set of formally identical protests ultimately robbed of any external referents and thus quickly deflected (cf., Kemnitzer n.d., Magdoff and Dolgin n.d., Marcuse 1964).

In the late 1960s, however, it was, as the JDL manifesto put it, in the name of "civil order and obedience" that league members guarded the streets of Brooklyn, initiated legal action against planned open enrollment at the City University of New York, escorted teachers to work during the school strike, and conducted a trenchant crusade against the 1969 candidacy of incumbent mayor John Lindsay. In affiliating with the cause of "civil obedience," JDL delimited a set of foes including black activists, radical students, and opponents of the Vietnam war. On one level JDL only manifested in new form contradictions long extant within and between Jewish communities of New York City and between those communities and groups of non-Jews. In solidarity with each other at one instant, the Jews of New York were in clear antagonism at another; particularly, variant Jewish immigrant groups had long reacted ambivalently toward one another. JDLers, unlike previous groups of Jews who were marginal within the larger Jewish community, could successfully appropriate, and had not hesitated to use, American forms of protest. Members of the league participated in several Events in the late 1960s that, themselves revelatory of ethnic and racial antagonisms (between blacks and whites, between Jews and blacks, between

Jews and Jews), quickly defined a "history" in terms of which future events could be constructed, rationalized, and understood.

These events were aspects of the animosities directly occasioned by the situation of the 1968 teachers' strike. In December 1968 a poem, written by a fifteen-year-old black girl was read on the radio station WBAI's "Julius Lester Program" by Leslie Campbell, a black teacher[17] who had taught in Ocean Hill-Brownsville. The poem, called "Anti-Semitism: Dedicated to Albert Shanker" (President of the United Federation of Teachers), began: "Hey, Jew Boy, with that yarmulka on your head / You pale-faced Jew boy—I wish you were dead. . . ." Matters were exacerbated when in January another participant on one of Lester's shows suggested Hitler "didn't make enough lampshades of them." JDLers, demonstrating before the radio station with signs of urgency—"No Auschwitz here"—had come to insist upon an issue that had increasing support from other Jewish organizations. The station answered the protests: yes, the poem was anti-Semitic but represented sentiments important within parts of the black community of New York City, sentiments about which the station declared itself obliged to inform its listeners, for the presentation of existent bigotries (racist and anti-Semitic) would contribute to their attenuation. JDL, and others including the UFT, the Anti-Defamation League, the New York Board of Rabbis, and the Workmen's Circle, achieved few explicit changes in WBAI's stance—the station did propose the reinstating of a program about the Jewish community—and a bitter contest ended as Event. In the same January (1969) JDLers also joined remonstrations against the Metropolitan Museum of Art for having included what was seen as an anti-Semitic introduction, written by a black teen-ager, in

[17] After the poem was read on WBAI, Albert Shanker, President of the United Federation of Teachers, called for the dismissal of Campbell, who had previously been suspended from his junior high school teaching job and reinstated by a state panel.

the catalogue to the exhibit "Harlem on My Mind." The introduction asserted that the Jew not only "exploited" blacks but that "Behind every hurdle that the Afro-American has yet to jump stands the Jew who has already cleared it . . ." (quoted from Weisbord and Stein, 1970). Part of what was seen as anti-Semitic here had been paraphrased from Glazer and Moynihan's *Beyond the Melting Pot*; in the paraphrase had come a shift in meaning. The catalogue, having become a *cause célèbre*, was eventually withdrawn from the exhibition by the museum.

The articulated interests of the particular group, the JDL, found a journalistic forum in these first few years— in the sense of a space for the communication of JDL activities and a corroboration of JDL analyses—in the *Jewish Press*. This paper, claiming a readership exceeding 100,000, covered the details of everyday life in Jewish neighborhoods of New York City, the neighborhoods from which JDL's first members came, as well as national and international news relating to Jews. That Meir Kahane worked for the *Press* at the time of JDL's creation meant an open channel of communication to JDLers and potential JDLers through the paper.[18] Kahane has even specified that his own initial commitment to the need for a Jewish defense organization had grown from his reading of letters to the *Press* detailing the difficulties of life for the Jew living in the inner-city: this contextualization immediately focused the domain of discourse (and of "need"). The league's defense was concretized against a mixture of groups, people, and things, including crime, "black and leftist anti-Semitism" and the "radical right."

[18] JDL's first advertisements in the *Jewish Press* set a tone familiar to readers of the paper: "We are talking of Jewish survival." "Are you willing to stand up for democracy and Jewish survival?" The group, first calling itself the Jewish Defense Corps, soon changed "corps" to "league," as the connotations of "corps" seemed overly "militant." It was, however, not coincidental that the groups organized by Vladimir Jabotinsky (see below) in post-World-War-I Palestine to protect Jewish settlers from Arab attack were named the Jewish Self-Defense Corps.

By autumn 1968 JDL listed over 1,000 members and 6,000 by the end of 1969.[19] Terms for a formal organizational structure[20] were promulgated, chiefly by Kahane, who, despite the explicit plan for roles and offices within the league, consistently stood to JDLers for the whole of their group. JDL chapters soon formed throughout New York City and outside the city as out-of-towners pleaded for a visit from the "Reb." The movement's growth was consciously ad hoc with any expression of interest or agreement snapped up and, if possible, converted into a new chapter.[21] In late 1971

[19] The largest membership reported by the league was 15,000 in 1972; that figure included all members, active and nominal, throughout the United States and in several other countries.

[20] The league's formal structure entailed "chapters." As portrayed in JDL's "Movement Handbook" (put out in 1972), a chapter was to be:

the unit in which JDL programs are carried out. Chapters meet at least once a month for educational purposes and to discuss past and future activities (p. 45).

A "national coordinator" was described as responsible for the selection of "district coordinators," under whose authority lay a specific number of local chapters and who, theoretically, chose chapter heads. At the top of the movement's outlined authority structure was the "executive board," headed by the "national chairman"; with Kahane's emigration in 1971, Zweibon became national chairman, and Kahane "international chairman." The executive board held direct responsibility for several "special groups" including a "squad" (discussed in chapter 3) formed for local "street" defense, and was followed in the league's official structure by a "national administrative board" composed of fourteen "desks" including area coordinators, membership, education and research, neighborhoods, finance, *aliyah* [immigration to Israel], youth (college and high school), overseas Jewry, political activities, women, defense, publicity, and national administrative board coordinator ("Movement Handbook," p. 43).

From its supposed inception, JDLers evinced constant dissatisfaction with this (or any) sort of organizational structure though many, indeed most, JDLers continued to claim that some sort of formal structure was necessary.

[21] Though JDL chapters were established in over a dozen U. S. cities, the most significant from the perspective of the "national office" in New York were those in Los Angeles, Chicago, Washington/Baltimore, Philadelphia, and Detroit, but none manifested the numbers or the energy

Kahane moved to Jerusalem, where his wife and four children had settled several months earlier. Although he spent every other month of the next year in the U. S., his immigration to Israel signalled the end of a mode of activity for JDL in the U. S.—of apparently unlimited energy and publicity; the signal was not fully believed for another year. After Kahane's departure explicit functions and clear lines of authority became the metaphor of necessity for JDLers, though they never adhered to the delegated divisions of task. Daily affairs were conducted by several score people, with "leaders" often drifting off after a few months: the formally outlined organization was paralleled by actual combinations of authorities and functions only insofar as "important" JDLers were quickly given titles and, if necessary, replaced with equal rapidity. By 1970 JDL had intensively become a youth movement; several dozen young JDLers spent summers between 1969 and 1971 at the league's camp in the Catskills, where practice in riflery and karate was combined with seminars in Jewish history, American Jewry, anti-Semitism, and practical "leadership training." And it was mostly these young JDLers who, willing to be militant and to be arrested, provided the core around

---

of the New York City chapters. Degrees of affiliation between these chapters and the national office differed from city to city, fluctuated over time, and were never officially specified, though they were all, at least in part, financially independent. Within non-New York City chapters, members debated their stance toward and standing within the national movement, with conceptions of the New York City league varying from a "main office" to a distant model for local activities. In January 1971 the chairman of the Boston chapter, Marvin Antelman, broke with the league and created the Jewish Survivalist Legion, characterized by Antelman as "militant and law abiding at the same time" (the *Rhode Island Herald*, April 2, 1971). In addition to these chapters, JDL set up groups on college campuses, claiming several score college chapters, although the large majority remained inactive. Flurries of JDL activity actualized in several other countries including Canada, France, England, and Belgium. After fall 1971, the league had "international" headquarters in Jerusalem.

which the Events of JDL's "struggle for Soviet Jewry" took form.

In assuming as their own the cause of the Jews of the Soviet Union, JDLers gave evidence of their proclaimed universalism—"for all Jews." The league thereby attained scores of new members and received world attention, but concomitantly the sense of the particular conditions of the original membership became ever the more blurred. JDL members, inspired by Kahane, were conscious of the modes of activity likely to be noted; the tactic became the impersonation of specific tactics that would give an image of militancy to the league. The following paragraphs outline the sense of escalation that accompanied JDL's activities in the name of Soviet Jewry by noting several, and far from all, of the league's "actions."

Late December 1969 found from a few dozen to hundreds of JDLers, depending on the hour of day or night, camped on East 67th Street in Manhattan, outside the headquarters of the Soviet Mission to the United Nations. With this first "100-hour vigil," JDL's struggle for Soviet Jewry had begun in earnest. During the day the demonstrators chanted and marched; in the evenings Kahane led seminars on Torah; then JDLers tangibly understood that, as one young JDLer put it, "he could lead us into hell if he decided to go down there." On December 29 the temper of JDL's program emerged when league members raided the Soviet news agency Tass and the travel agency Intourist, painting *"Am Yisroel Chai"* ("the people of Israel live") on the walls and wreaking general havoc, while in a simultaneous action other JDLers at Kennedy Airport handcuffed themselves in protest to a Soviet plane just arrived from Moscow.

"If the Jewish Defense League has indeed used violence against the Soviet Union and its American puppets, it is," wrote Kahane in 1970, "because for 53 years there has been an agreement to try the respectable way. The result has been almost total decimation of the Jewish community within the U.S.S.R. from a religious and national standpoint (the *New*

York Times, July 9, 1970).[22] For JDLers, their motto and refrain "Never Again" took on new solemnity as they apposed the "spiritual" peril of Soviet Jews to the physical destruction of European Jewry in the 1940s. In fact, during this period JDL's analysis of its situation, explicitly now set apart as Ideology, became more and more separated from the everyday lives of league members, becoming an abstract, though evocative, portrait of the True Jew.

Activism became manifest among Soviet Jews themselves after the 1967 Israeli-Arab War, an activism brought to international attention in the last month of 1970, when eleven persons were tried in Leningrad: two were sentenced to death and nine to long terms of labor in Siberia; the eleven, nine of them Jews, had admitted intentions to escape by hijacking a small Aeroflot plane. The two death sentences were commuted to prison terms after pervasive protests from Jewish and non-Jewish organizations, newspapers, and diplomats. By the early 1970s most American Jewish groups gave verbal, and later physical, support to the struggle for Soviet Jews, though never with the intimations, allegations, or realities of JDL militancy. During the month of the trials in Leningrad, there were demonstrations for Soviet Jewry in Rome, in Tel Aviv, in Washington, and in New York, where JDLers held their second 100-hour vigil at the Soviet Mission to the United Nations.[23]

Early January 1971: The league's spontaneity coalesced in a heyday of recognized activism. JDL suggested a boycott of U. S. companies trading with the U.S.S.R., had members

[22] In the 1950s and early 1960s, Kahane himself rejected illegal or militant reactions in aiding Soviet Jewry; he has, however, pointed out to people noting this rejection, that by 1964 he was writing in the *Jewish Press* that the Student Struggle for Soviet Jewry deserved credit for its active protest for Soviet Jewry.

[23] During the week of the vigil JDL formed "Student Activists for Soviet Jewry," officially distinct from the league and unimportant except for its representations of the league's efforts to broaden appeal and acceptance and increase its flexibility in setting up sub-groups not officially acknowledged as part of the league.

phone Soviet agencies and residences in the U. S. throughout the day and night, "harassed" Soviet diplomats in New York City, and seemed, in what they presented as their "aim," to be "threatening detente." When the *New York Times* reported that a spokesman for the Soviet Mission accused JDLers of having uttered "the dirtiest four-letter words in the Russian language" (*New York Times*, January 12, 1971), they impressed even themselves. On January 8 a bomb exploded outside the Soviet cultural building in Washington, D. C. during the early hours of the morning; minutes later a caller informed press services of the explosion, continuing: "This is a sample of things to come. Let our people go! Never again!" (*New York Times*, January 9, 1971). In what was becoming a familiar scenario of responses,[24] Andrei Gromyko registered official ire with the U. S. ambassador in Moscow; the U. S. State Department extended apologies to the Soviet Union; American Jewish groups denounced the bombing, calling it unJewish; JDL

[24] In June 1970 almost thirty JDLers were arrested when members of the league invaded the Soviet trading company Amtorg. A pipe bomb went off in November at the Intourist and Aeroflot offices (located in one building in Manhattan), causing some damage to the building, including broken windows. Telephone callers to Associated Press and United Press International connected the bombing to the trial, about to take place in Leningrad, saying "Let the world know that while the Jews are on trial in Russia, the Soviet Union will be on trial," and concluding with "Never again" (*New York Times*, November 26, 1970). Representatives of the league, including Kahane, disclaimed knowledge of the explosions but applauded those responsible, suggesting that violent protest for Soviet Jewry would probably occur again. American Jewish groups condemned the explosions; representatives of the Nixon administration called the bombing a "senseless, criminal" act (*New York Times*, November 26, 1970); in late November Golda Meir was reported to have said that violent activities against Soviet properties in the U. S. were "acts of utter irresponsibility that were morally reprehensible, and worse still, sabotaged organized efforts to secure the rights of Soviet Jewry. . . ." (*Jerusalem Post*, November 29, 1970). In early 1971 a brick was thrown from a passing automobile into a window of the Intourist and Aeroflot building. Again, JDL denied involvement.

refused to condemn the explosion and refused to concede complicity.

Kahane announced an "indefinite moratorium" on harassment of Soviet personnel by the end of January, after the league had been informed of a grand jury investigation of four cases.[25] The moratorium was short-lived. Demonstrations continued. In March a thousand league members and supporters were arrested when they blocked traffic near the Soviet Mission in Washington D. C. JDLers, prideful in having sustained an image of militance through numbers, boasted, as one JDLer put it, that there was not jail space "in the nearest fifty counties" to house those arrested. And now, said Kahane, since JDLers "sat in the streets singing *Am Yisroel Chai* [The people of Israel live] . . . all the police know the words and the music."

Although JDLers teased that "full membership" required "at least one arrest," indictments for major offenses were a different matter, as JDLers learned that spring and the next fall with two sets of serious indictments against league members. On September 8, 1971, seven JDLers were charged with bombing Amtorg (the Soviet trading company) the previous April. Almost in relief, and in fear, attentions were turned to the "legal defense" of these seven young JDL members,[26] providing a mode of action containing the ex-

[25] The four cases involved an invasion of Amtorg in June 1970, an explosion in November 1970 at the building housing Aeroflot and Intourist, demonstrations outside the Soviet Mission in December, and an alleged offense against Dr. M. T. Mehdi of the Action Committee on American-Arab Relations.

[26] One of those indicted in connection with the Amtorg bombing had been arrested the previous September (1970) for allegedly planning to fly from New York to London to hijack an Arab plane there in reprisal for an earlier hijacking attempt against El Al, the Israeli airline. He was sentenced to five years in prison for passport falsification (the maximum sentence) but was deported to Israel in spring 1972, several months before the trial of the "Seven" took place. Two of those indicted in the fall of 1971, plus another unidentified person, were also charged with having attempted to bomb the Soviet Union's residence in Glen Cove, Long Island (June 1971). The Glen Cove

citement of contest and the security of legality: the protest was located as one against government "persecution." "What Have the Seven Done?" asked a JDL leaflet: "They picketed, protested, and got arrested for their brethren in the Soviet Union—and for this they are on trial today. . . . we fear that pressures from the Soviet Union, from Arab countries, and from other interests may prejudice their trial."[27]

The indictments against the "Seven" followed arrests in May 1971 of a dozen JDLers, including Kahane, charged with conspiracy to violate provisions of the Federal Gun Control Act of 1968.[28] At pre-trial hearings in 1971 in the Eastern District Court of New York there was a disposition of the case with Kahane and two other defendants pleading guilty to one of two counts.[29] Scores of letters were mailed to the court before sentencing, many echoing JDL's contention that the only illegality had been the league's having neglected to obtain a $250.00 tax-stamp before exploding a bomb at Camp Jedel in 1970; the bomb was described as having been made, following instructions in a Black Panther

---

estate was also the object of an alleged bomb conspiracy for which four JDL members were arrested in May 1972; of these four, two received prison sentences in November 1972.

[27] The trial was held in September 1972; three of the defendants pleaded guilty, one to conspiracy to bomb and to make bombs, and the other two to illegal possession of dynamite.

[28] The defendants were charged under Title I of the Gun Control Act, concerning the transportation of firearms across state lines, and under Title II, concerning legal procedures requisite to making firearms. A thirteenth person was named as co-conspirator but not as defendant.

[29] The disposition involved a reduction of the indictment to one count and the dropping of charges against all but the three defendants who pleaded guilty. At the pre-trial hearings the legality of government evidence, obtained through wiretapping JDL offices, was contested by the defense. Under the assumption that the wiretaps might have been illegal, the judge inquired whether the government could prove its case without that evidence, and learned that an undercover agent who had infiltrated the league would testify against the defendants.

manual, to indicate to JDL summer campers the "serious-
ness" of "extremist" groups. At sentencing, Judge Jack B.
Weinstein explained this as a misapprehension:

> We do not have here merely a technical failure to pay a
> tax on the making of a demonstration bomb on private
> property. Rather what we have here are conspiracies to
> illegally obtain many guns and to illegally transport them
> across state lines; we have here conspiracies to illegally
> obtain many sticks of dynamite and great quantities of
> gunpowder and other explosives and to store much of this
> material in crowded areas at great danger to the innocent
> public—and then presumably to use them (U.S.A. v.
> Chaim Beiber et al.).

The sentences imposed were suspended, surprising JDLers
who had amassed for the witnessing of Kahane's martyrdom.[30] Soon after the sentencing, Kahane departed for
Israel, a departure symbolic, if not absolutely causative, of a
new period of uncertainty, even inactivity, within JDL. Protests for Soviet Jewry continued, but remained for the most
part unnoted by news media. During Kahane's stays in the
U. S. that year plans were drawn, activities posted, but with

[30] Kahane was fined $5,000 and sentenced to "5 years imprisonment
with execution suspended and probation for 5 years" (U.S.A. v. Chaim
Beiber et al.). The maximum sentence for the crime to which Kahane
had pleaded guilty was $10,000 or five years imprisonment or both.
One of the other defendants was fined $2,500 and given a three-year
suspended sentence with probation; the third, an eighteen-year-old,
was fined $500 and sentenced to a three-year probation. Stipulations
attached to the sentencing forbid the defendants to become involved
"directly or indirectly with guns, bombs, dynamite, gunpowder, fuses,
molotov cocktails, clubs, or any other weapons" (ibid.).

In May 1972 Judge Weinstein increased the stringency of the "special
conditions" of Kahane's probation after the court decided that Kahane
had violated the original probation conditions by aiding the dissemination of information about weapons in Brooklyn during August 1971
(U.S.A. v. Meir Kahane).

Kahane was eventually sentenced to one year imprisonment for
violation of probation in early 1975.

his departures interest plummeted, dozens of members disappearing for another month. Two Events occurred that fall and winter, suggesting to JDLers, grown tired with spontaneity's lapse, a hope of reinvigoration. Each of these Events occurred apart from the everyday lives of JDL members, who learned about the occurrences through news media; yet the public mention of JDL returned the drama of everyday life as well—marking JDL's enormous dependence on the media. The first of the two Events reviving images of the actualization of JDL militancy came in late November when four shots were fired through an eleventh story window of the Soviet Mission. The Soviet representatives' claim that four children had been sleeping in that room only augmented the sense of drama. As one young JDLer put it, "When George Bush [U.S. delegate to the U.N.] told Meir we were hurting detente, then we knew we were finally getting someplace."[31] The U. N. General Assembly debated the incident in acrimony for hours, and JDLers loudly, publicly, and as often as anyone would listen, denied involvement. Soon the incident lost its power in recitation, press coverage dimmed, and JDLers again spoke bitterly of a "media blackout . . . imposed by the City." Explosions at Sol Hurok Enterprises and Columbia Artists in late January again brought note. Both companies had previously been the objects of JDL sit-ins and protests for serving as booking agents to Soviet performers appearing in the U. S. Telephone callers to news services informed: "Cultural bridges of friendship will not be built over the bodies of Soviet Jews. Never Again" (*New York Post*,

[31] Within a week, a young JDLer was arrested and charged with having bought the rifle (under a false identification) from which the shots had been fired into the mission. JDLers described the arrest as an "obvious frameup," since, they claimed, throughout the day when the rifle was said to have been purchased, several hundred people saw the accused at religious services. Charges were dropped in February 1972, and another person, previously a member of the league, was charged with having presented false identification papers in buying the rifle.

January 26, 1972). Over a dozen people were injured in the explosion at Hurok's offices; a secretary died of smoke inhalation.[32] For the first time JDLers, faced with the possibility of league activities having resulted in murder, were ambivalent, and for the first time a vocal segment of JDLers suggested to each other that the league had not been involved or that, if the bombs had indeed been placed by JDL members, these persons had acted independently. Of course, very few JDLers ever knew, in fact, whether the league had or had not been responsible for particular acts. Immediately upon hearing of the explosions many JDLers were dissatisfied and then angry when Bertram Zweibon— "national chairman" since Kahane's move to Israel—postponed a press conference for several hours. "That," said one league member, "is just what causes suspicion. . . . If Meir was here he would have seen the press right away." For weeks—until Kahane returned and called them foolish—a contingent of middle-aged JDLers stayed away from the league office in Brooklyn in fear that they would be observed by city police or federal agents and implicated in the bombings.

In the next months, conceptions of JDL were transformed from ethnic imagery toward metaphors of nationalism; the struggle for Soviet Jewry had provided the ground in which this shift could occur. Moreover, Soviet Jewry had indeed become the cause of "all Jews," and in that, JDL's own program was attenuated. The next summer (1972) Camp Jedel in the Catskills was discontinued, to be replaced by a "leadership training school" in Jerusalem—a manifestation

[32] Four JDLers were arrested the following June in connection with the firebombings. Charges were dismissed against two of the defendants in June 1973 when the other two and another witness (all JDLers) refused to testify. One of the witnesses was granted the right not to testify on the grounds that illegal government wiretaps had been used against him. The other two were held in contempt of court for claiming they could not testify because Jewish law forbids testifying against another Jew in a secular court of law.

of the refocusing of league concerns around *aliyah* and toward Israel.

Late in summer 1971 JDL announced the opening of an "International Office" in Jerusalem and the adoption of *aliyah* as the core of league ideology. Within the larger movement, even within JDL's executive board, this shift brought opposition: wasn't JDL formed, asked many members, exactly because Jews had finally decided to "stay and fight"? Curiously, JDL's apparent success, its renown, and its failure—especially its inability to sustain an analysis of the concrete, problematic situation of its membership—combined to make Zionism a successful alternative. Zionism was to be taken in earnest; in contrast with previous decisions not to demand a unified, official stand on issues occasioning disagreement within the membership, the Zionist ideology was, said JDL's leadership, to be espoused by all members.

Revisionism, the Zionist faction with which JDL aligned itself, was ideologically nationalist rather than socialist, a nationalism that JDL increasingly based on a grand metaphysical, and eventually messianic, scheme. The revisionist movements, sired by Vladimir Jabotinsky in opposition to the official Zionist Organization, developed between the issuance of the Balfour Declaration in 1917, in which the British government promised the creation in Palestine of "a national home for Jewish people,"[33] and the independence of the State of Israel from British rule in 1948. The Revisionist Party, founded in 1925, resulted from Jabotinsky's dispute with the Zionist Organization, a dispute that centered around proper strategies for ensuring the creation of a Jewish state. Since that time, revisionism has spawned a set

[33] In a white paper of 1939 Britain rescinded what had been seen as the original intention of the Balfour Declaration, by denying plans to create a Jewish State. But more devastatingly for European Jews on the eve of the Nazi holocaust, the paper restricted Jewish immigration to Palestine to 75,000 persons over the succeeding five years.

of groups and parties, politically rightist, intensely nationalistic, and favoring militancy as a political tool.

Despite its affiliating with revisionism, the sort of *aliyah* JDL proposed differed from historic precedents in being a proletarian, blue-collar immigration allied *against* socialist aspects of Zionism, and in being a migration from a country where the majority of Jews felt welcome and "at home." JDLers, not in full consciousness, masked the unique character of the *aliyah* they were developing—particularly its proletarian origins—in stressing dramatic analogies between the situation of Jews in America and that in the Europe from which the early revisionists had come, and by stressing similarities between JDL and the revisionist movements at the expense of JDL's own specificity. JDL's association with revisionism, though hardly surprising, is important for understanding the opposition between JDL and the established Jewish groups in America as well as that between JDL and the government of Israel. Although the reality of Israeli politics today is in many ways closer to early revisionism than to the socialism of the first kibbutz dwellers, the ideological split remains, has become reified, and is taken to be a serious (and thus "real") difference by contemporary Israeli and diaspora Zionists. Named in the 1920s, the opposition intensified in the late 1940s with terrorist tactics against British rule in Palestine of the revisionist Irgun, or National Military Organization (cf. Hertzberg 1972, Laqueur 1972, Schechtman 1961, Sykes 1965). Menachem Begin, Jabotinsky follower, once commander of the Irgun and founder of the opposition Herut (Freedom) party in Israel, now a member of Knesset (parliament), is, along with Jabotinsky, Theodor Herzl, and Max Nordau, a revered "hero" to JDLers.

Jabotinsky, born in Odessa, Russia, helped the Jewish self-defense groups in that city during the 1903 pogroms and was in large part responsible for creating—and especially proud of—the Jewish Legion, which during World War I fought against Turkey as part of the British war effort in

Palestine. Also, in 1923 he developed the youth movement called Betar from a small student group in Riga, Latvia, calling itself Histadrut Trumpeldor (Schechtman 1961). The name Betar, honoring in acronymic form (in Hebrew) Yoseph Trumpeldor, killed in 1920 defending a Jewish settlement in Palestine, also recalls the last site of Bar-Kochba's resistance against the Romans in the first century —at the fortress Betar. A curious and pondered figure within Zionist history, Jabotinsky has been viewed less negatively by anti-revisionist Zionists than have other revisionist leaders. Chaim Weizmann, the first Israeli president and one of Jabotinsky's early opponents, wrote that Jabotinsky,

> the passionate Zionist, was utterly un-Jewish in manner, approach and deportment. When I became intimate with him in later years, I observed at closer hand what seemed to be a confirmation of this dual streak; he was rather ugly, immensely attractive, well spoken, warm-hearted, generous, always ready to help a comrade in distress; all of these qualities were however overlaid with a certain touch of the rather theatrically chivalresque, a certain queer and irrelevant knightliness, which was not at all Jewish (Weizmann 1949, as quoted in Laqueur 1972).[34]

[34] Joseph Schechtman, who has written an extensive biography of Jabotinsky and was active in the revisionist movement, accords even the negative parts of Weizmann's characterization a truth with which Jabotinsky, who himself declared he had a "goyische kop" (non-Jewish head), would not have been the last to agree. The following description of Jabotinsky by his non-Jewish admirer Count Michael Lubiensky is worth quoting in that it represents a view with which JDLers are in agreement, a view that indicates truth in an oft-repeated assertion that Zionism was an ideology of assimilation rather than the opposite (cf., for example, Arendt 1970):

> You know that I hold Jabotinsky in highest regard and that my opinion of Weizmann is trimmed accordingly. But as I see it Dr. Weizmann has all the chances to retain the allegiance of the majority of the Jewish people. Because his entire mentality is identical with that of an average ghetto Jew, while the mentality of Jabotinsky is spiritually nearer to me, a Gentile. I understand him better; he

Early on Jabotinsky had been influenced by Italian socialism, later becoming anti-socialist on the grounds that the
new Palestine settlements should not expend energies on
internal class conflict. With Jabotinsky claiming to be a
simple Zionist, neither socialist nor capitalist, revisionism
in fact mover farther and farther away from organized labor
(Laqueur 1972), Those who call Jabotinsky a fascist refer
particularly to the unmitigated militarism of Betar members
and to a group of neo-revisionists in Palestine (1930s), the
Biryonim (zealots), led by Abba Achimeir, who appropriated Italian fascism as their ideological model and whom,
despite disagreements, Jabotinsky continued to support.

Of the organizations engendered within revisionism, Jabotinsky had a special relation with the youth movement
Betar. According to Jabotinsky's biographer Schechtman
(1961:405), there "was a fascinating, almost mystical, association" between Jabotinsky and the members of Betar. And
it was Betar that became a model for young JDLers who saw
themselves a continuation of Betar's aim: "to create a new
generation of Jews, a generation which is proud, fierce, and
which values freedom and honor more than life itself"
(Katz, n.d.). Though hesitant to equate anyone with Jabotinsky, the young JDLers gingerly suggested that Kahane,
in his relationship to them, resembled "the great man."
Large parts of JDL's formal ideology were culled directly
from revisionism. Among the "five principles" of JDL
Ideology, *"hadar"* (pride), the second principle, was the
fountainhead of Jabotinsky's conception of Betar members.
The politics of JDL's nationalism were posited years before
in Betar, dedicated to the creation of a Jewish state with
"more Jews than non-Jews; for the first condition of a national state is a national majority" (*This is Betar* 1952);

---

evokes in me a kindred response. For a ghetto Jew he is, on the
contrary, too simple, too direct. He will be listened to, applauded,
but he will be followed only by those who have overcome the ghetto
complex (as quoted in Schechtman 1961:554).

"legionism" ("military training"), "discipline," and *hadar*" were, for Betar, the necessary means. *Hadar*, wrote Jabotinsky, combines

> various conceptions such as outward beauty, respect, self-esteem, politeness, faithfulness. . . . *Hadar* consists of a thousand trifles, which collectively form everyday life. . . . More important by far is the moral *Hadar*: you must be generous if no question of principle is involved. Every word of yours must be a word of honor, and the latter is mightier than steel . . . (as quoted in Schechtman 1961: 416).

Kahane's own father, Rabbi Charles Kahane, had known Jabotinsky, and as a boy Meir had belonged to Betar. In the late 1940s when the British colonial government was sharply limiting immigration to Palestine, Meir Kahane participated in a demonstration against Ernest Bevin, who was visiting the United States as British Foreign Minister. Betar has maintained chapters throughout the Jewish diaspora; during times of apparent failure or inactivity within JDL, members joked, "Whenever JDL starts in a city, two months later there's a big Betar chapter."

When Kahane spoke in the United States during the winter 1971-1972, he insisted on Zionism and *aliyah* as the only alternatives to the eternal hazards of the diaspora. Kahane consciously accentuated the "negative reasons" for emigration to Israel, for the "positive reasons" were not deemed "enough to get people to go":[35]

[35] I quote this speech (recorded by myself in Englewood, New Jersey, late 1971) extensively because in addition to delineating JDL's position on the diaspora and on *aliyah* it illustrates some of the mechanisms behind Kahane's success as a public speaker. Much is lost when the speech is transposed into written form, since Kahane's use of tone and accent is central; yet, from this excerpt, one can see how Kahane manipulates categories and then re-asserts them; the "taken-for-granted" is turned on its head to resurface at a slightly different angle, often humorously and on the precipice between the familiar and the unordinary. Within Kahane's speeches, the interplay of imagery and

[Today in the U. S.] many problems are laid at the feet of the Jew. If there are racial problems, it's the Jew— drugs, the Jew—generation gap, the Jew—earthquakes, the Jew. Always the Jew. . . . There's a growing economic problem—inflation on the one hand, unemployment on the other. . . . A person who has had a good job for twenty years and a home and a car is not easily willing to give this up. . . . And so what we find in our days . . . is a shift . . . on the part of Middle America to the right. The Birchers grow and the American Nazi Party grows. And even those people who don't join them begin to think' some of what they say is true. . . . Busing is being used by the radical right to poison the minds of America.

Kissinger! . . . Nixon finally has one Jew and he sends him to China!—and the Kissinger trip is being used. Every radical right leader has the real reason, and it's a Zionist plot to convince China to fight Russia. Halavay! [if only it were so] . . .

Let us not be fools. Let's not repeat the mistakes of Jews in a certain country which in the 1920s had a Jewish foreign minister . . . whose constitution was written by another Jewish cabinet minister . . . where Jews felt secure and free and safe and above all equal. Equal. And in Germany when Adolf Hitler first arose, they laughed

---

"truth," of religion and common sense happens quickly. As one image is absorbed and responded to, another is presented. He employs cliches in unusual ways. Yiddish phrases appear in contexts where they do not seem to belong but where they are comprehensible to any listener. Toward the end of Kahane's speeches, his audiences often clap, even where applause does not seem appropriate, laugh, even when laughter is (almost) out of place.

Kahane conducted seminars for JDL members in "public speaking," and although his phrases and format could be copied, the results were only quasi-successful, since Kahane's sense of his audience, his timing, and his playing back and forth between his words and the audience response are not easy to emulate. He pushes the audience toward exclusion and then inclusion, emphasizing the American Jew's mistakes (*this* Jew in *this* audience), and then appears to offer options.

at him and said, "How many members does he have? How many people follow him?" Or they would say, "He doesn't mean us; he means the *ostjuden* . . . the Eastern Jews; he doesn't mean us." Nevertheless, he did. And the impossible happened there—that which could not happen. . . . So, what is *this*? Nazi Germany? No, it isn't Nazi Germany, and it isn't Czarist Russia, but neither was Nazi Germany Czarist Russia. . . .

I believe that the ultimate solution to the Jewish problem will not be found here or in any country—except one. . . . For 2,000 years we prayed and we wept for Zion. On *Tisha b'Av* our great grandfathers sat on the cold stone, by flickering candles, and they wept for *shivat Zion*—the return to Zion. . . . For 2,000 years Jews would be buried in Poland, or in France, or in Yemen with a little bit of earth from the land of Israel. . . . Today El Al is ready to take you there. And the Jewish Agency will pay for it. . . .

The argument was blatant: anti-Semitism is unavoidable when Jews live among non-Jews, in non-Jewish lands. The sharp rejection of Kahane's "negative" Zionism by representatives of other Jewish groups (including the American Jewish Committee, the Synagogue Council of America, and the World Zionist Organization) and by most liberal American Jews, was, like JDL's position, sustained through arguments recalling insecurities (such as the fear that American Jews could be faced with and accused of the old conundrum "dual loyalty"). In effect Kahane's liberal critics accepted the terms of his debate. In 1972 an article by Kahane appeared on the opinion and editorial page of the *New York Times* (May 26, 1972) calling for "massive emigration to Israel." "G-d forbid," wrote Kahane, "that it should happen again. The moment of truth is upon us and may we act with the courage and resolve so needed at this time." The response of many liberal Jews with whom I spoke about the article is epitomized in the hastily spoken words of one New York

City psychiatrist: "I suppose he's right . . . but he shouldn't say it so publicly."

For American Jews "normalization" was pictured through Israel's being constructed as a home of national origin, a land like the lands from which other Americans had come. In this, as in JDL's plea for *aliyah*, identity was fitfully built on the historicization of an abstract future. JDLers from the start constituted themselves as marginal, while simultaneously calling themselves central, authentic, mediators among Jews. While, from this contradiction, there came a certain power in the United States, a power possible in a day of "ethnicity," the limitations were different in Israel, where JDL began to minimally organize in 1971. In September signs in English and Hebrew were posted on billboards in Jerusalem, inviting "all students who are JDL members or who wish to join" to a meeting "to plan the JDL program in Israel." Support came from young Americans, most of whom had been JDL members in the U. S. JDLers stipulated that the league would become a "bridge" between opposing political, social, and religious interests, remaining outside the domain of State politics.[36] To paraphrase one JDL leader:

> We'll never become a political party. That's fine for those who want to sit in Knesset. . . . We'll do things like work among the poor and educate all Israelis . . . to know

[36] During the winter 1971-1972 the league started arranging for a JDL kibbutz and a *kiryat* (town) in Israel and began seeking applicants for a JDL school to be established in Jerusalem. The school, designed to train JDLers in leadership skills and to teach courses in such areas as league ideology, Jewish history, and anti-Semitism, was expected to open on a year-round basis by June 1972. The students were to be obligated to return to the U. S. for two years to work on college campuses as "Jewish Mark Rudds but without the violence"—to create active college JDL chapters, dedicated to both *aliyah* and the defense of Jews in the diaspora. The plans were altered for lack of funds and applicants; a leadership training course was given in Jerusalem during the summer 1972 and was attended by about twenty young JDLers from the U. S.

they're Jews first, not just Israelis. We're for all Jews . . .
whether they're religious or not or Sephardim or Ashke-
nazim, or a member of any party.

JDLers were particularly satisfied with one of their first
"actions" in Israel when students at the summer school
(1972), joined by a few other JDL members in Israel,
amassed in the city of Hebron on the West Bank, demanding Jews be given state permission to settle there. (Although
a Jewish community had been established in adjacent Kiryat
Arba, the Israeli government did not allow Jewish settlement in Hebron.) Israelis were less positive. "We don't need
them here," concluded one student, who had attended the
first meeting of the league in Jerusalem. "We don't want
it—neither the government nor the people. Why did he
[Kahane] come here? . . . We don't want their military
patrols or anything else. . . . For Israel they don't have
answers."

In autumn 1972 Kahane, contradicting his earlier stance,
announced the creation of a political party ("*HaLiga*"—the
League) and himself a candidate for election to Knesset.
Elections were held in December 1973, two months after
the fourth Israeli-Arab War. Kahane did not win a Knesset
seat. The "ethnic model" and the form of action JDL tried
to create around that model were not viable in Israel, where
the dialectic of absorption was conditioned and encompassed by the tangible antagonism between Israel and the
Arab states.

CHAPTER II

Motionless Dance

"IF," writes Sartre, "it is true, as Hegel says, that a community is historical to the degree that it remembers its history, then the Jewish community is the least historical of all, for it keeps a memory of nothing but a long martyrdom, that is, of a long passivity" (1965:66-67). Since Sartre wrote these words other modes of historic identification have emerged for the Jew with, particularly, the re-creation of the State of Israel; but still, Israeli politicians, for instance, bemoan (or occasionally justify) a fear, a certainty, or at least an awareness of a "Massada complex," represented through images of the last Jewish defenders in first-century Palestine, who preferred communal suicide at Massada to capture by the Roman invaders. For JDLers, however, Jewish History[1] became the primary medium through which Jewish "heroism" could be asserted, explained, and posed as "natural." Massada was not, for JDLers, the symbol of a "complex," but of a courageous, militant defense against anti-Semitism.

For JDLers, it was shared History that held together the disparate mass of the league's symbolic constituency—all Jews, "whatever they look like, wherever they may be." This History has something to do with "common ancestry" but is a specification insofar as the jump from ancestry to history entails a limiting of the permutations linking relationship through "blood" and relationship through "code for conduct." These terms have been proposed by David M. Schneider (1968) for characterizing how people are related

[1] Throughout this book the notational form "History" refers to JDL's version of the ancient Jewish tales, many of which are from the Old Testament.

to each other in American kinship: one is either a relative through birth, that is by blood or through code for conduct, that is, by law, or through both (e.g., the illegitimate child is a relative through blood, the spouse through law, and the son or daughter through the two). Schneider has suggested that these same relationships may structure the domains of religion and nationality so that American religion, nationality, and kinship are structured similarly (Schneider 1969). JDLers did not tend to use the words "blood" and "code for conduct" to characterize the commonality they impute to all Jews—although "blood" *was* sometimes used—but they often spoke of the "family of Jews," "Jewish ancestry," and "Jewish action." Through History JDLers indicated the preferred relation between "being Jewish" and "acting Jewish."

The process through which JDLers constituted their identity cannot, however, be understood outside the broader context of Western stratification, in general, nor, as noted above, outside the apparent phenomenon of "emerging ethnicity" in the United States in the late 1960s and 1970s, in particular. That JDL, with some success for its own membership, could try to authenticate almost any set of league actions as prototypically Jewish, or, inversely, that JDLers were labeled "Jewish panthers," was not the simple consequence of flexibilities inherent to Jewish (or any) History. But rather, these phenomena must be viewed in terms of the options offered for self- (and group-) identity within the context of class and ethnic stratification in the West, options in terms of which JDL's version of Jewish History was itself, of course, created.

Some answers come from comparisons outside the American or Western tradition, and it is well to begin with those comparisons. Louis Dumont, the Indologist, has contrasted the holism of the caste system, where structured totality is paramount, to the individualism of Western society, where individual substance ("blood") takes precedence. Dumont (1970) suggests that in the Western universe, with an egalitarian ideal, certain people are placed apart on the basis of biological criteria. And the ideal is thus sustained. Yet the differences between an ideology of hierarchy, as in caste India, and an ideology of equality, as in the United States, are not unbridgeable. The "ethnicization" of a South Indian caste has been described by Steve Barnett, and this case—a shift between one universe of meaning and another—serves as a particularly illuminating background against which to understand the system of American stratification (Barnett 1971). Barnett cites the example of one non-Brahman upper caste that experienced a shift in the meaning of blood from code for conduct to natural identity. As the result of such a shift, a caste becomes one unit among a number of units vying with each other for power and status (i.e., an ethnic group) rather than part of a structural religious system that attains meaning at the level of the whole. The admission of ethnic "equality" allows the possibility of reference group behavior since behavior and rank are no longer synonymous. Individual action in the context of ethnic groups, Barnett points out, does not necessarily imply rank. Members of any ethnic group can appropriate distinctive behaviors and actions of any other group without necessarily effecting alterations in relative rank between the groups involved. Furthermore, with Western stratification (e.g., ethnicity), orders of group ranking become preeminently debatable. This sort of analysis is relevant to the process by, and the extent to, which ethnic and racial groups can, so to speak, improve their lot; how far do new labels go (how far can they go)?

Soon after the beginnings of the civil-rights movement in the early 1960s, American ethnic and racial groups initiated the escalating process for seeking separate identities and distinct rewards. (Clearly, the motives and conflicts were extant long before the civil-rights movement, but in that struggle the needs and contestations were given new form.) The question still is, however, escalating into what? How much of the process is being rechanneled, even if under new labels and new laws, into modes of interaction that are as old, perhaps, as the Puritans? The very fact of reference group behavior, characteristic of the class (and ethnic) system of "equal" substantialized units, can become inimical to profound alteration. Once the form of struggle is established, it can be appropriated by any group. As a result the same modes of action can be used in the effort to produce radical transformation and in the effort to sustain the status quo.

JDL offers a key case for analysis here since the group seemed, variously, to have wanted to both preserve the state of things and effect profound alteration. JDL labeled the New York City police force in terms competing with the least polite epithets of the radical left; yet it rejected Lindsay in 1969 and McGovern in 1972, favoring in each case the more conservative candidate. The league upheld a traditional Judaism while trying to re-do the essence of the American Jew. JDLers spoke before the American left and the American right and received as much condemnation and applause in one quarter as in the other. As JDL's protests grew from local concerns to entail wider and wider issues, and as the league became a "public" phenomenon (acting for the "public" through the media), JDL began to look more and more like other activist groups. Indeed, any activist ethnic group must at once prove capable of using the sorts of demonstrations and actions and ideologies that prove that that group is validly and distinctly ethnic.[2]

2 A series of advertisements for Rheingold beer (produced in the late 1960s by Doyle, Danne, and Bernbach) well illustrates the use and creation of ethnic substitutability. Each advertisement in the series focused around a group of "ethnics," partying and enjoying themselves with Rheingold beer. Everyone, the advertisements proclaimed, could actualize his/her distinct ethnic identity through Rheingold beer— Poles, Jews, Germans, Irish, blacks, and Italians—everyone, that is, except the WASP, about whom Rheingold produced no advertisement. The advertisements were almost identical except that Rheingold beer seemed to cause the Italians to say "Mama mia" with increased authenticity, while Poles were made to dance a better polka (and so on for each "ethnic" group). The advertisements were deemed a failure (Della Femina 1970). The distinctive authenticity offered each group through the beer was apparently negated when viewers saw that all

"Emerging ethnicity," the public presentation of inequality or difference and demands for rectification (as the
potential for assimilation *or* for separatism), can be turned
into a self-defeating process. While differences (in treatment) remain intact, the claim that there is equality, that
the egalitarian ideology is manifest in fact, can become ever
the more insistent, since "obviously" anyone can become an
ethnic. The gap between the egalitarian American ideology
and the actual relations among people appears to diminish
when similar forms of protest create the illusion of equality
among all groups. As forms of protest are themselves replaced by other forms—almost any other—opacity increases
ever the more. "The distance between facticity and Idea,"
writes Marcuse, though in a somewhat different context,
"has increased precisely because they are conceived of as in
closer relation. . . . The history of idealism is also the
history of its coming to terms with the established order"
(Marcuse, 1968:192). While ethnicity seemed to become *the*
internal position, the preeminent mode through which
Americans could define themselves and their group, the
medium through which that identity was expressed went
beyond any particular ethnic or racial group, becoming an
ideological paradigm within which anyone could (must?)
find a place. In short, the symbolic forms through which
ethnicity can be made known and defined are commutable
between ethnic/racial groups; moreover, any one form (or
"tactic") is expendable in favor of another. Eventually all

---

the "Others" were equally authenticated. It is instructive to compare the
Rheingold advertisements with those for Levy's rye bread, which were
an astounding success. Picturing members of different "ethnic" groups
enjoying the bread, the advertisements read (or said): "You don't
have to be Jewish to like Levy's." Here, the (Jewish) content becomes
available as form through which any ethnic group can stress the
authenticity of its own distinctive ethnicity. Substitutability is re-
enforced, while it is simultaneously masked in the double move from
(apparent) content to (apparent) form. (I am grateful to John Kirkpatrick, Richard Kurin, and JoAnn Magdoff for reminding me of this
series of advertisements.)

"ethnic" identity, thus denuded of historic referentials, appears, in David M. Schneider's phrase, to be composed of "contentless symbols." This process can pertain not just to ethnicity but to any potential form of group identity in a situation of individualism, where the group is understood as analogous to the individual.

The form absorption (cf., Marcuse 1964) has taken in the individualistic West is aptly characterized by Henri Lefebvre: "A system of substitutions emerges where every compendium of meanings—apparently independent and self-sufficient—re-echoes another in endless rotation" (1971: 51). In the sentence just quoted, Lefebvre is considering technicity in everyday life (e.g., gadgets) and more generally, "modern" notions of rationality—rational bureaucracy, rational behavior, rational analysis. Lefebvre suggests that everyday life has become ("almost") irretrievably cut off from anything else; based on an ideology of individualism, "disguising and vindicating the society's basic character" (1971:69), everyday life is the sphere, par excellence, for domination and manipulation. Everyday life (which is, of course, where people spend most of their time) attains meaning through difference and through quantity: the system of substitutable differences according to which everyday life is lived masks the fact that difference, itself, has become but another kind of similarity; nothing can be said, and the only choice is how to say it. (Compare Althusser [1969] on contradiction and overdetermination with Barnett [n.d.].) Talking of fashion, Lefebvre writes:

> You can "say it" with clothes as you can "say it" with flowers: Nature, Spring, Winter, evening, morning, mourning, parties, desire, freedom—the "system" makes use of everything including adaptation that becomes fictitious and make-believe; anything can be said—or nearly anything. Successful coupling is a matter of authority that can impose whatever it chooses—or almost; in some cases, it is true, "almost" prevails (1971:119).

What Lefebvre sees as the modern mode of living the quotidian through endless substitutions—"terroristic" because based in nothing beyond itself—has also found its place in *ethnic* living (or "almost"). Symbols through which internal positions are constructed can be speedily appropriated by any group (and when anyone can be a "panther," let us say, the meaning of panther has been diluted beyond recall). This process is ever the more complicated since the articulation of ethnic internality is, in large part, establishing a position vis-à-vis other ethnic groups: new symbols (equally substitutable) are created with increasing rapidity. Additionally, ethnic groups have explicitly taken on "everyday life"; correlative to the ethnic tactic is the naturalization of life-style, the definitional provision for modes of living that are "naturally" ethnic. (A commutable natural life-style, defined through ethnicity, begins to look preeminently cultural.)

The escalation of the ethnic tactic is the necessary counterpart to substitution (absorption), but it is a race against time. Once a tactic is created, publicity, through media in particular, begins the process of deflection through appropriation. (Yet, activist groups themselves seek media attention as one of the few means by which to "get the message across.") Protest becomes absorbable (Marcuse 1964) in the act of being heard at all. Ideologies of ethnic activist groups opposing the "ruling ideology" are undermined by the substitutability of the tactic since other—any other—apparently similar groups appear, countenancing the ruling ideology and thereby nullifying the possibility of "critical" internality.

In the remainder of this chapter I will describe the basic terms of JDLers' identity, the processes through which JDLers attempted to construct that identity, and the sorts of conflict and contradiction that developed therein. The most basic split in JDL's characterizations of its universe was that between Jew and non-Jew, but once that split was made, a series of other alternatives were superimposed upon this characterization; for instance, both a Jew and a non-Jew can dislike Jews—in the one case becoming a "self-hating Jew" and in the other an anti-Semite. The problem ultimately became one of deciding who was internal and who external to JDL's situation, but since "internality" and "externality" (Sartre 1963)[3] may be in conflict depending, for example, on whether they are defined through stress on blood or on code for conduct, complexities evolved. As JDLers tried to think and act their way through these complexities, basic definitions and categorizations were themselves shifted.

JDLers defined themselves through a progression of nested identities: the individual JDLer, JDL, American Jewry, Americans (Jews and non-Jews); in the abstract, this basic JDL scheme remained constant: each level was related to the level preceding it and the level following it in an analogous way (through, that is, the relation of part to whole). The series of nested identities appeared to be harmonious with each other, and, additionally, the scheme could be filled in by any (ethnic, racial, religious) set of identities (cf., Gordon 1964). Yet somewhere along the line there was a vital shift for JDL between a population potentially able to be mobilized and a population seen as unmitigatingly Other. The extremes could be identified; the large middle was internal or external depending on context and design. JDL posited a shared "authenticity" in behavior, manifest, league members suggested, in JDLers' similarity to Historic heroes. Yet clearly, all American Jews did not enact JDL's model of "code for conduct." Rather, JDLers consciously equated JDL behavior and strategies

[3] Jean-Paul Sartre's *Search for a Method* (1963) approaches the anthropological question (of Self and Other) through a basic process of mediation between internality and externality, a mediation whereby the two can be dissociated or joined, contrasted or compared, opposed or themselves mediated. This book is constantly (although tacitly) informed by Sartre's work.

with other American activist groups: "We are Jewish Panthers," they proudly proclaimed. Given the series of increasingly inclusive relations, structured by the opposition between Jew ("Jewish hero") and non-Jew (at the extreme, anti-Semite), JDLers were immediately beset with a plethora of conflicts and contradictions; generally, manifest conflicts were handled through ad hoc rearrangements that, for the moment, at least, masked the essential contradictions. In characterizing those Actions that made for an authentic Jew, for instance, exclusions become more important for JDL than inclusions; that is to say, the identity of the group (JDL, the Jew) was often defined more by what it excluded than by what it included. In addition, behaviors and beliefs the league wanted to exclude (or include) were defined differently from various points of view. In separating the Jew from all Others, certain exclusions were stressed. In the most untenable case, the exclusions themselves became mutually exclusive. Here the nested identities (individual/JDL/Jew) were torn apart.[4]

JDL, in short, attempted (though not in these words) to use a distinction between form and content to attain maximum flexibility in situating itself vis-à-vis relevant Others. If, for instance, a tie or association was made between JDL and another American "ethnic" group (e.g., with the Italian-American Civil Rights League), it was possible to maintain separation (as Jews) by declaring that forms intermingled while contents remained distinct. Or, taking another case, the league tried to establish its ultimate identification with all Jews, despite apparently opposing forms (e.g., forms of "action") on the basis of content ("blood"), which, however, composed other forms. To put it another way, JDLers, in intentionally varying their appositions of form and content, tended, through their history, to move from the concrete to

---

[4] The problem may be akin to the mediator that needs a mediator that needs a mediator and so on; mediators can be conceptualized, but in action, they may be irreconcilable, one unto the other. Often an earlier conception of JDL identity could not be sustained.

the abstract and to hide that process. This process was part and parcel of JDL's decreasing attachment to the actual situation of its membership and its increasing analysis of the abstract ("authentic") Jew. That authentic Jew was, however, held up as supremely real.

The effort to be all things to all Jews while remaining this (or that) kind of Jew was fated to succeed, at best, only momentarily and only by fiat, since the universalistic claims in combination with particularistic interest were undermined when form and content refused to hold their own. "The dialectic of action," writes Martin Silverman, "is the dialectic of form and content" (n.d.:1). It is precisely the insistence of form in becoming content and of content in becoming form that makes it possible to *think* this is that and impossible to sustain the thought.

For instance, JDL set up an explicit dichotomy between "image" and "identity" (the first, appearance; the second, essence). Image entails those activities necessary for "defense" but undesirable for internal permanence, such as extreme militance. Although this separation was conceptually comforting for JDLers, as it appeared to preserve essential identity from the incursions of "necessary" action, the boundaries of the domains in terms of which image and identity were posited as being separable could not be a priori delineated. These boundaries were far less clear in fact than in concept; concomitantly, what was merely image at one time became identity at another and vice versa. Identity and image (content and form; form and content) erupted in paradox. These distinctions would seem to have granted JDL the possibility to "maximize its options" (cf., Silverman 1969); in fact, they were the foci around which contradiction became manifest. Succeeding chapters of this book present concrete illustrations; at this point I shall only deal with some possible results of such paradox.

One mode of action, given mutually exclusive images and identities, is enacting the paradox itself. Both (or all) images are taken up and the categories of thought become the (self-defeating) inconsistency of action. For instance, if a JDLer acts like an "establishment" Jew, there is a failure to separate JDL from diaspora Jewry. On the other hand, if a JDLer acts like no "Jew" would ever act, that may be too new (i.e., non-Jewish). JDL's distinction between image and identity assumed that appropriate contexts for each sort of behavior—behavior that was only image and behavior that was truly Jewish—were isolatable and controllable. Image and identity were set up as context dependent, but context invariably gets in the way. To be a bit too simple: What do you do when aspects of both contexts—the Jewish "establishment" and the anti-Semite, say—are present at once? And they always were—in the actor who bridged them, if nothing else. Exactly the dichotomy (between image and identity) posed by JDL as a (conceptual) way out emerged in action as a contradiction from which escape appeared increasingly unlikely. This contradiction is similar to the "double-bind" analyzed by Gregory Bateson (1972) and applied to group behavior by Martin Silverman.[5] The egalitarian Western universe ordains that people become what they do, but since the assumption is that even from the internal position each individual is capable of understanding (absorbing) any other individual, anyone *can* do anything (cf., Barnett 1973a, 1973b, Dumont 1965a, 1965b); for this reason *ex*clusions are vital to group self-identifications. The

[5] I am grateful to Vincent Crapanzano of Queens College, CUNY, for his insights on the problematic character of the double-bind as used in Bateson (1972), where it is akin to a rhetorical figure applied to a psychodynamic process. Similar questions as to the character of many psychodynamic features are given one answer in Jacques Lacan (1966), where the structure of language is held *to be* the structure of the unconscious. My use of the double-bind is as a mechanism through which to characterize historic relations between people and groups. Those relations do not inevitably follow the relations of language or ideology; this point is emphasized in that the double-bind in regard to JDL is applied to a group of people almost intentionally appropriating their own reification in endowing created History with substance— and thus veracity.

danger is that the actor really *may become* what s/he does (image, it appears, has almost inexhaustible potential for enveloping identity). When what is *done* explicitly includes mutually exclusive modes of action, then the insertion of image into identity becomes inconsistency of Self. In action, identity is no longer immune from the actualizations carried out in the name of image.

"There will be a break-down in any individual's ability to discriminate between Logical Types whenever a double-bind situation occurs . . ." (Bateson 1972:208). Bateson describes how a (therapeutic) "patient's" responses to the double-bind situation—where "winning" is not possible—may become general forms of reaction (schizophrenia). One answer within this situation (though hardly a way out) is the trans-lation of meaning (of demands, threats, desires, goals) away from literalness, so that symbolic people in fictional contexts are used to say what cannot otherwise be said. Obviously, the situations of the double-bound patient and the double-bound ethnic group are not identical. In particular, as is true for most people, double-binds occur, but they are not the only form of interaction. The patient's recourse to metaphor does, however, show certain similarities with JDL's evocation of categorizations based in the metaphoric domain of History. JDL's version of Jewish History, form-ing the core of the movement's Ideology, was a moderniza-tion, if you will, of that very ancient past that Albert Memmi called "too splendid, too remote as a matter of fact, too far past, with no continuity with what we are today . . ." (1962:202). It is, wrote Memmi, "the past of the Bible, of the Passage through the Red Sea and of the manna in the desert. Since then nothing—or almost nothing" (1962:202). Through "blood" and through "code for conduct" JDL made that "too remote" past contemporary, and the means by which this occurred was backward metaphorization of the present. While the blood tie between the Jew and his/her mother, the tie which makes a person a Jew, is a "na-tural" tie, the link to Moses and Abraham, to Judith and

Deborah, is a tie of metaphoric blood; the mediator between the "natural" blood of the family and the metaphoric blood of History is "code for conduct" (conceived by JDLers as "action"). Part of the essence of what the Jew should be is to behave like a Jew, so that behaving (JDL said) like Moses or Judah Maccabee behaved was to establish a "chain" wherein blood became available through code for conduct. (An apparent stress on "action" tended to mask a heightened significance attached to blood, for if substance could be defined through action, then substance bore both the weight of "blood" and of "code for conduct.") Along with code for conduct, joining the blood of mother and the blood of "Moses," was land. "Each one of you," said a JDLer urging settlement in Israel, "had an ancestor who touched the rocks of that land. Not in Dizengoff Square [an area in modern Tel Aviv] but in Shchem and Hebron [both on the West Bank]." The league explicitly defined its activist stance (and its "actions") as authenticated through, and as a continuation of, the History of the Jewish people. Action, that is, was substantialized—a phrase itself suggesting contradictions inherent to a situation where action is consciously based on ethnicity.

Image and identity could be kept apart through (a version of) History, for in History identity could be secured as genuinely Jewish, and image justified through the (metaphoric) recall of Moses and Massada. But this could only work for a moment out of time. Quickly, the aim became the enacting, the continuing of that History: the metonymization of metaphor.[6] JDLers not only claimed that their

---

[6] See chapter four for further discussion. Definitions of metaphor and metonymy used here are from Seitel (1972). Seitel defines these terms as follows: "Metaphor, in the most general sense, is the relationship which obtains between entities of separate domains by virtue of the relationship each has with entities in its own domain" (1972:29). "Metonymy, in the most general sense, is any relationship which obtains between entities by virtue of their mutual inclusion within the same domain" (1972:32). Both quotations are underlined in the original.

behaviors were like those of Moses and Deborah, that their actions bore similarity to Bar-Kochba at Massada or Judah Maccabee before the Greeks, but that these behaviors and actions were identical. That which began as merely analogical became reified in the claim that JDL actions and ancient Jewish History were one and the same. As noted above, for JDLers, league action was substantialized, this substantialization occurring exactly through the metonymization of metaphor. When History is viewed as a metaphoric domain, symbolisms from that ancient History can be applied comfortably, even if provocatively, in contemporary identifications: they remove the form of relationship to unassailable representation (for what does it matter if they are assailed?). But as metaphor, consciously relayed as myth, History lacks the power of contiguity and the import of veracity. The placement in contiguous time, the metonymization of metaphor, where the merely similar becomes the literal foundation and essence, *is* the revitalization of the "too remote" History about which Memmi wrote. It is a revitalization that endows History with meaning and at once removes the harmony attending a merely metaphoric past. When History is reified and grounded within an order of natural things, when Moses and Massada are taken from the realms of legend and made the natural beginnings of a process producing JDL, then the problems of the present are no longer resolved in the past: they now belong to the past as well.

That ancient History, however, is a "metalanguage" anyone can interpret. The symbols around which it is built are not private but part of the cultural baggage, if not the ultimately meaningful beliefs, of every Westerner, never mind every Jew. This is, in fact, another difference from the schizophrenic's metaphor: this metaphor appears immediately relevant and interpretable. Even with History metonymized (made contiguous and thus "real"), the contents of History can be used to answer dispute. This answering, however, may itself be paradoxical since once

History is part of the present (they are in one contiguous domain), it is no longer a separate referential system, alike but not *of*. The uses of this History partake of the more general tension between metonymy and metaphor (Jakobson and Halle 1971, Seitel 1972). In particular instances (and in the short run) JDLers could even make use of that very tension between History as metaphor (and thereby removed from conflict) and History metonymized (the present as well as the past). A JDL activity or aspect that was criticized was compared to an episode from History. Initially, the comparison appeared metaphoric, often funny (e.g., Moses not forming a committee to study the grassroots of Egyptian anti-Semitism). Once the similarity (on whatever level) was accepted (an acceptance often signaled through applause or laughter), it was de-fictionalized: this is how things *really* were (and are) in that history you all accept.

Frequently, the Historic parallels were used/created in reference, specifically, to JDL behaviors and beliefs belonging to the (labeled) domain of ethnic activism. Often the question was explicitly posed: "What makes you different? You are militants, not Jews." Given the militance of the Other, answered JDLers, the Self (the Jew) cannot survive otherwise, and furthermore, the ability to be militant when necessary is part of traditional Judaism (for who would deny that Moses was a "traditional" Jew). But this answer reveals the tension between metaphor and metonymy, the tension between a link proven in metonymy and justified in metaphor. For eventually, anything becomes possible. Jews can act their Jewishness in any way at all: What JDL does *is* Jewishness.

Scholar/Chaya

AT its inception JDL was composed of lower-middle-class adults, concerned primarily with the personal hardships of everyday life. Although Kahane had just published a book dedicated to the "enslaved Jews of Russia," the members of JDL were far more alert to the "Jewish problems" in Crown Heights and Williamsburg than to those in the Soviet Union. In 1968 there were no JDL seminars on "Jewish history" or "Jewish identity": these were hardly at issue. Yet by the early 1970s the league was receiving headlines in major newspapers throughout the U. S. for its "militant" campaign against the Soviet Union; the small and homogeneous membership had grown to include thousands of young Jews, many Jews who had never worn a yarmulka, even a few Jews from Long Island and Westchester (the symbolic bastions of the "establishment"); and there was scarcely a New Yorker who had not heard of "Meir Kahane" and "Never Again."

JDL's leadership was aware of the extent to which media attention was responsible for growth in membership and in prominence. The shift from an "adult" membership to a core of activist "youth," for instance, was encouraged with the media in mind. As noted above, Kahane and other JDL leaders have said that although Soviet Jewry might have become one of JDL's major concerns had JDL remained an adult movement, that issue received extensive media coverage because of the willingness of young members to demonstrate publicly and "loudly." Demonstrations were commonly planned consciously for media coverage, since only through media could people learn, in the words of one JDLer "about the important things, the things we do for

Jews all over the world." Yet JDLers, themselves, were in the audience of public viewers. During the evening news JDLers received an image of themselves, and although the activities viewed were often prepared for this very purpose, they attained a separate reality in being broadcast. Not only were JDL activities planned in accordance with a conception of what would appeal to the media, but these activities were thought of as fully enacted only if so recorded. Many JDLers who did not spend much time at the league office or were not involved in particular JDL activities received much of their information about the league (about themselves) from newspapers and television.

Media presentations took internal aspects of the league outside by telling the world about JDL and brought external events inside by providing JDLers with distilled "images" of themselves. Such coverage validated JDLers' self-definitions as part of an historical process since News was seen to contain the makings of history. Ironically, what was reaccepted as history by JDLers had been consciously designed and acted out by them to portray an image not necessarily reflective of identity and internal essence. The scenarios were, in large part, designed *for media attention.* And the images taken back, the images with the weight of history incorporated in their projection, were that much farther from identity, having been processed at least three times—by actor, broadcaster, and viewer. JDLers were aware that the projection of the league through public media ran the risk of absorption by the dominant society. Participation in history through evening news had to be conceptually reinserted into a Jewish History; that is, the American images had constantly to be transformed back into Jewish images in such a way that they were still attractive to American media.

By the early 1970s JDLers did believe that they had succeeded in becoming part of history, but this history was conceived as a history-in-the-making. Sagas of Jewish heroism offered legitimation but did not present concrete models for everyday plannings and interactions through which they could sustain the conjunction of American present and Jewish past. This chapter looks at the construction of JDL through examining the created relation between the Idea of JDL and the "organization," the relation between the reembodiment of a glorious History and the daily job of making JDL work. Modes of interpersonal integration within the league will be considered as well as the significance attached to that integration vis-à-vis contemporary Others (and vice versa). The chapter concludes by presenting the conception of intergroup relations that served as a symbolic construct for JDLers in situating themselves in the world and in acting to change that world. That symbolic construct was forged in relation to life in New York City, seemed to achieve an historic manifestation in the struggle against the Soviet Union, and began to break down with the shift to a nationalist ideology in late 1971 (with Kahane's settlement in Israel at that time). The construct, though not explicitly articulated by JDLers, served as a model for self-definition and for "Jewish" action in Gentile America.

Among JDL's explicit aims was the creation of a new Jewish image, an image *of* the Jew (held by non-Jews) and an image *for* the Jew (from the "Jewish" point of view). The designation "New Jew" was defined and set against the notion of "Old Jew." The JDL "Movement Handbook" (made available to JDL members in September 1972) places the New Jew in the context of the holocaust. The handbook reads:

> . . . a new philosophy was born as a new Jew arose from the mound of corpses at Auschwitz, Treblinka, and Buchenwald.
>
> From the ashes and decay of the holocaust comes the philosophy of the Jewish Defense League. An organiza-

tion of Jews whose hallmark is action. Nevertheless, that
action is based upon a philosophy—the philosophy of
the New Jew (p. 4).

The New Jew (exemplified by the JDL Jew) was not portrayed as unprecedented within the annals of Jewish behavior. Immediately the handbook contextualizes the New
Jew within the securest tales of traditional Judaism. About
the "philosophy of the New Jew" the handbook (p. 4) asks:
"Is it really new? Or does it draw from traditions and well-
springs of the Old Jew who once walked his land so proudly
and who loved his people so fiercely?" Generally JDLers
used the term "Old Jew" to refer to the vincible Jews of the
European ghettos. When emphasizing their own connections
with ancient "heroes," however, JDLers called Biblical
Jews (and themselves) Old Jews and the Jews of the diaspora
(with "galut [exile] mentalities"), New Jews. Or, sometimes,
the ancient Jews were called New Jews because, like JDLers,
they were posed as Jews of action. The Old Jews of the
European diaspora were placed in time between the destruction of the second Temple by Titus in 70 c.e. and the re-
creation of the State of Israel in 1948. They are characterized
by JDLers as Jews without a land, without a society of their
own, and without the political sagacity of self-interest.

The two poles against which JDL presumed to create itself
and to outline its activities were the "helpless" Old Jews of
the diaspora and anti-Semites, the perversity of the ultimate
Other. The first task was geared inward, toward the education of the unenlightened Self; the second task was directed
outward against the opposed Other, a task discussed and
acted out in the language and method of physical confrontation. The two tasks were seen by JDLers as intersecting,
for the transformation of the Old Jew of the diaspora into
the New Jew (JDL) was taken, in its very name, as a weapon
against anti-Semitism—the actual combating of anti-Semitism was held to rely on the manifestation of the New Jew.
The concepts of the Old diaspora Jew and of the anti-Semite

were the referents of "Never Again": Never Again will the anti-Semite be able to exterminate the Jew and Never Again will the Jew be an "easy mark" for anti-Semites. Kahane described the meaning of Never Again on the Long John Nebel radio program (December 31, 1971) as follows:

> Never again means that we have had it in the concept of being beaten and not hitting back. No one will respect us, and no one will in the end love us, if we don't respect ourselves. . . . I have often said that when I've had contact with anti-Semitic groups—that it's got to be man to man. If it's not man to man, if you're not willing to have it on a man to man basis, then it again will be pig to pig, but never again will it be man to pig with us the pig.

The revitalization of History, the naming of the Jew's situation, and the diagnosis of dilemmas formed a framework for instilling the categorizations of the contingent present with additional import. A History must be constructed before it can be appropriated as "real," and within that space, the space between History and history, lay fundamental elements of JDLers' identity and consciousness. References to Judah Maccabee, the *shtetls* (villages) of Eastern Europe, Haman, or the Roman Titus sought their signifields (the characters and episodes to which they "really" referred) in the here and now, in the contemporary United States. The search for meaning was momentarily solved by JDL action, but action, once carried out, became Historical, or at any rate, it became analogous to History. There were moments when JDLers intensified analogies with other times and places until, for instance, Tsarist Russia and Nazi Germany and America (just tomorrow, if not today) were indistinguishable as equally *galut* (of the exile). At other moments the league attempted to establish itself and its era as singular and to press a likeness rather than an identity with Historic antecedents. At such times the "anti-Semites" and "Old Jews" with whom JDLers interacted were posed as *like* Haman and Titus on the one hand

and the populations of *shtetl* Europe on the other, but as not really the same. This choice enabled JDLers to use History as an analogous system by which to judge the present and as a source of personal identity *within* which JDLers were said to exist and in terms of which they could be characterized.

The "force" of History offers a means of scanning the present to delimit the "scope" of relevant thought and action.[1] The terms "force" and "scope" have been proposed by Clifford Geertz to designate, respectively, "the thoroughness with which . . . a [symbolic] pattern is internalized in the personalities of the individuals who adopt it, its centrality or marginality in their lives" and "the range of social contexts within which religious considerations are regarded as having more or less direct relevance" (1968:111-112). JDL's History was structured in terms of the antipodal concepts of Jewish heroism and anti-Semitism. This opposition was erected at the center of JDL Ideology[2] and provided its "force." Jewish heroes/anti-Semites were the extreme instances of the broader categories, Jew/non-Jew. This wider categorization extended the "scope" of Jewish hero/anti-Semite to include not only anything "Jewish" but also a great deal that was non-Jewish but was seen to effect Jews or Judaism, positively or negatively.

Jewish heroes and anti-Semites of History came labeled with their indisputable differences and their antagonisms. The force of the opposition between the two was not abated in JDL's present, even though the characters to whom and contexts in which the terms of the opposition could be ap-

[1] This dual, if not contradictory, directionality is not unique to JDL. Its interest here lies in the particular modes of reference to past, present, or future in terms of each other, in the ways in which structured time is appropriated within ideology. These issues are discussed further in chapter four.

[2] Paralleling the notational difference between History and history, "Ideology" (with a capital "I") refers to the formalized system of beliefs that JDL *calls* its Ideology.

plied were harder to discern. The anti-Semite was not merely defined as a being, but as a being-in-action against Jews. The New Jew (JDLer), therefore, could not just *be* a New Jew, but had to act vis-à-vis Jews and anti-Semites. The Jewish hero was defined as a Jew who acted against anti-Semitism, so the identification of the hero depended upon the identification of the anti-Semite.

The broader categorization, Jew/non-Jew, was not based on action. These were categories of being, and although "predispositions" toward certain types of action were correlated with that being, the distinction did not rely on behavior. (See chapter five for a discussion of such predispositions.) JDL expressly upheld the Orthodox interpretation as to *who* is a Jew. According to religious law, a Jew is either the child of a Jewish mother or someone converted to Judaism through the prescribed procedure of *halakha* (religious law).[3] One is either a Jew or one is not a Jew; there is no possibility for an intermediate condition. JDLers defined their movement not to contradict the "pure domain" (Schneider 1968) of religion. The league, however, not only included but actively sought "secular" Jews: these people were expected to respect the laws of Orthodoxy but not necessarily adhere to them in private. In general, the "pure" religious domain is extremely difficult to isolate even analytically, and perhaps more so in Judaism than in Christianity, given the potential sociocultural inclusiveness of Judaism along with the absence of a formalized system of religious authority. For the extremely Orthodox Jew almost every aspect of daily life is considered and enacted from a religious perspective. JDL *did* demarcate a domain of "pure" religion (though JDLers did not use that word), which included fundamental prohibitions and prescriptions of Judaism (e.g., the observance of *kashrut* and of

[3] This designation coheres with David Schneider's proposal (1969) that the structure of religious or national identification is similar to that of kinship and is based on identifications of "natural identity" through blood or of law through code for conduct.

Shabbot and other holidays). Orderings and decisions with respect to contemporary society and politics were, for the most part, said to be outside the domain of Orthodoxy. In this way it was possible for JDLers to insist on their adherence to Judaism even when acting in ways which the *Rabbonim* (Orthodox teachers and rabbis) condemned as contrary to Jewish law. The *Rabbonim*, said JDLers, have primary authority when it comes to rules of *kashrut* and religious observance, but in the arena of politics "what we say is just as right as what they say."

For many JDLers, particularly those who were not religious, the effect of preserving religious identification while acting-as-a-JDLer was reversed. The fact that JDL subsumed certain religious laws and assumptions into *its* Ideology became the point of significance. The primacy of religious authority was replaced by the superordinance of JDL Ideology. Many young JDLers, for instance, began to observe the laws of *kashrut* because JDL Ideology sanctioned such observance. JDLers, religious and non-religious, assumed Judaism to be their encompassing identity, but it is the significance and meaning of *Jewishness* rather than Judaism with which JDL was concerned. In the construction and enactment of Jewishness the relation to the non-Jew bore greater stress than the relation to God or to the laws of Orthodoxy. The History from which JDLers created their identity is basically the divine History of the Old Testament, but for JDL the stress was not on the relation between man and divinity; it was on the relation between the Jewish people and anti-Semitism.

JDLers saw themselves as representing Jews as opposed potentially to all non-Jews. At this level, the inside community, defined through being, was the widest Jewish community, and the outside community that of the non-Jew. Distinctions between inside and outside were additionally proliferated from the perspective of the intra-Jewish community. Here the quest was toward sub-typification within a domain of similarity and in terms of *action*. At the more inclusive level JDL's task was explicated as one of separation and at the intra-Jewish level one of mobilization toward ultimate fusion.

The league variously stressed (a) the conjunction of JDL with all Jews and (b) the distinctive orderings and activities that made JDL different from the self-denigrating, weak Jews of the diaspora. These two faces coalesced for JDLers in the Historic heroes who provided models of the "Jewish fighter" within an "authentic" Judaism. The struggle to construct a self-identity in accordance with this model was both a theoretical and a practical concern. Myths of Jewish heroism were a facile medium for the expression of an idealized Self, but the day-to-day organization of the move-ment, the development and sustaining of authority patterns and role differentiations, of projects and interactions with Others carried Biblical symbolism into the arena of daily decisions and formulations. The past provided a model of the desired present, and, equally, the present informed as to notions of the past.

One of the key symbols through which JDLers con-structed their movement, in thought and in action, is a term referring to one of the sub-groups of the league, a sub-group formed for physical defense against "anti-Semitic" activities, and called the *chaya* squad. *Chaya* is a Hebrew word meaning animal and, generally, wild animal.[4] The chaya squad was headed by an individual, appointed

[4] Two common Hebrew words can be translated by the English word "animal": *chaya* and *behema*. Although the exact usage varies from the Biblical to the Talmudic to the modern period, *chaya*, while often understood to include *behema* within its meaning range, tends to imply wild animal in contrast to *behema*, which refers to domesticated animals. In modern Israel it would be an extreme insult to call a person a *behema*; the connotations would be fat, lazy, and above all dumb. *Chaya*, depending on the context, could be insulting or com-plimentary when applied to a person. (For use of these words during the Talmudic period see Jastrow 1903.)

Although *chaya* is a Hebrew word, it will henceforth not be itali-cized in the text since it is used by American JDLers as part of everyday English speech.

by JDL's general leadership. The members of the squad were selected according to criteria of physical prowess and were expected to attend training sessions in physical "defense" including karate and riflery and to be available for "street action." Responsibility for carrying out the consequences of JDL's dictum that anti-Semites had to be dealt with physically before anti-Semitism could develop into a large-scale movement, fell particularly to the chaya squad. Premises behind that dictum were illustrated to a JDL leadership class in Ideology when the teacher said, "Had Hitler been assassinated in 1924 millions of Jews and non-Jews would be alive today." The chaya squad, more than most of JDL's subdivisions became a coherent, continuing group, with a relatively stable set of general aims and purposes.[5]

The squad was set up in the early 1970s to assume the functions of a JDL division called the oz-ers—*oz* is a Hebrew word meaning strength. The oz-ers were disbanded by JDL's leadership due to diminishing internal "organization." Significantly, the chayas were supposed to differ from the oz-ers in not being accorded an "elite" position within the league. (This change was indicative of a more general shift in JDL, which will be discussed shortly, from the valorization[6] of individual members to the valorization of JDL as a whole.) To members of the league, chayas represented the unique quality of their movement among Jewish

[5] I am specifically dealing with the circumscribed period of time during which my fieldwork was carried out. Named categories employed by JDL such as the "chaya squad" changed rapidly. Many of the specific terms and usages discussed did not exist six months earlier or six months later. They were, however, posited within a general framework of greater duration.

[6] Following English translations of Dumont, I use "valorize" to indicate the level of normative order, the level of social "value"; the valorization of the individual stipulates the individual person to be the locus of value. In a culture where individualism is the dominant ideology, the key metaphor in terms of which groups and relations are conceived is the individual.

groups—active strength for Jewish "defense." The squad was taken as the extant substantiation of the mythologized scenarios around which JDL was originally formed. For people who characterized JDL as "fascist," "un-Jewish," or "vigilante," elements of the same scenarios formed the basis of the condemnations. For JDLers, it was a very different story: the making of a Jewish Defense League "history"[7] stemmed from the telling and re-telling of the league's earliest exploits. By 1972 JDLers who had joined the movement at its inception would sit in the league office ruminating about the days when JDL was "nothing." The "early days" were talked about and romanticized as if there were decades in between. To paraphrase one JDLer who considered himself an original member, speaking before a meeting of JDL youth in late 1971:

> It's suddenly fashionable to be in JDL, but it wasn't like that when we started. How many people in this room were ever asked to get up at 5:00 in the morning? [About half of the fifty or so people in the room indicated that they had.] Wait. Wait. And then asked to go to some street corner to meet a fellow you'd never met before in your lives? Or had forty posters to give out and when those forty were used up went to the garbage pail where people had thrown them to use them again? We used to say to a guy, "Read this. But stand right here and give it back to me." Because we didn't have enough paper to print hundreds of leaflets or any place to print them. How many of you were ever surrounded by 250 angry cops and there were 7 of you and you had to get in there and look brave? . . .

The "history" of the movement was not just a fact out there but the beginnings of a legend, integrating JDL with the History of Jewish heroism. Frequently when JDLers engaged

---

7 When used in quotations, "history" is history on its way to becoming History, as JDLers seemed, *in fact*, to become Jewish heroes.

in an activity of which they were particularly proud, at least one of the participants would proclaim, "It's just like '68 all over again."

As the movement expanded with the conscious attempt to establish a stable organizational structure involving different individuals carrying out a variety of tasks, an ambivalence developed about the kind of growth desired. The choice was posed by JDLers as one of "quality" versus "quantity." Quantity meant continual enlargment of membership, so that in the words of one JDLer, "If there are 1,500 people to call for an action, at least 300 will come." The option of quality implied the dismemberment of what was referred to as the movement's bureaucracy, since quality suggested "spontaneity" and "action." The advocation of quality was based in the desirability for JDLers of returning to the (already mythologized) character of the league as it was in its first months.

These choices did involve definite decisions about the organizational structure of the movement. For instance, in May 1972 JDL's executive board promulgated a series of organizational changes involving a redefinition of criteria for membership and some modifications in the channels of authority and formal interaction.[8] Official revisions in the

[8] The revised structure included the following changes: the semi-autonomous nature of the "youth movement" was given up, and all membership positions were opened to "youth" and "adults" on an equal basis, with the tasks of organizing in high schools and on college campuses re-defined as one of the fourteen areas under the National Administrative Board. At a meeting held in Brooklyn—with separate meetings held in each of New York City's boroughs—to inform the members of these changes, the JDLer leading the meeting said that if the "best person" to hold a certain leadership position were a nineteen-year-old, that person would get the job, but if the "best person" were an eighty-five-year-old, that person would. The spirit of this statement was in contrast with the then existent importance of youth and the youth movement, an importance that had increased steadily during the preceding several years. A distinction was set up between JDL "members" and JDL "supporters." Before being granted the full rights of membership, a prospective JDLer would have to undergo a three-

organizational structure of the movement made little difference in the daily workings of the league. They were attempts to encapsulate the Idea of JDL within a workable format, to embody the extraordinary, the heroic and the unique, on the one hand, and the everyday, the stable, and the typical, on the other, within one movement.[9] Contrast between the heroic and the everyday did not in and of itself result in perceived choice or conflict. In the abstract almost any JDLer envisioned the ideal actualization of both possibilities at once. But the effort to make the quotidian extraordinary and the heroic an everyday phenomenon succeeded only fleetingly; the gap between these fleeting successes and the ongoing failures, the gap between the desirable and the actual, created and manifested incessant re-definings and new orderings.

The concept of the chaya represented the idea of the heroic and its everyday manifestation. Conceptually, the notion chaya served as a link with traditional heroes of Jewish History through similarity (i.e., shared substance and shared behavior), and with the contemporary anti-Semite through antagonism (i.e., different substance and

---

month probationary period. During this time the participation of potential members in JDL activities would be observed; they would be expected to read specified books and articles, and their "background" would be investigated. The last requirement was an effort to curtail, if not preclude, the infiltration of the movement by the government. Supporters were not to be held responsible for all the obligations of membership, including regular attendance at JDL activities and a yearly $100 donation, but were not to be eligible for leadership roles within the movement. A program was also described requiring all JDL members to participate on a weekly basis in "ideological and education discussions and seminars" ("Movement Handbook," p. 39A).

[9] The concept of the routinizing of charisma is of obvious relevance to this discussion. What I want to emphasize here is not the fact of routinizing but the processes of definition and growth of this particular movement that entailed routinizing and innovative transformations together, "reformulations" and "new steady states" simultaneously (Wallace 1956, Weber 1968).

opposing behavior). Chaya referred to a tangible group, involved in concrete activities, and to any JDLer, whether or not actually a member of the chaya squad, who acted like a member of the squad was ideally expected to act. For instance, when a young JDLer who was not a member of the squad carried out a particularly dramatic demonstration against the Soviet Union's treatment of Jews at a Soviet artistic performance in New York City, and was arrested, he was said to have "become a chaya." One active JDLer said of him, "He is finally a chaya. He's been just on the verge for quite a while, even before he became so active in JDL. Now he's really made it."

The selection and use of the specific word "chaya" was a conscious attempt to name the New Jew, the incarnation of the ancient Old Jew. The term stood for JDLers in explicit contrast to the image and reality of the Old Jew of the diaspora—an image and reality that JDLers wanted to transcend, to reverse. "The galut image of the Jew as a weakling," writes Kahane, "as one who is easily stepped upon and who does not fight back, is an image that must be changed" (1971:141). Conception of the chaya came to signify JDL as a whole in comparison to "weak" diaspora Jews. The notion of the chaya also carried meanings at less inclusive levels, where it stood in contrasting and/or complementary relationships with attributes seen as characterizing JDL, in the first place, and non-Jews—the Others—in the second place, before whom and because of whom JDL created itself.

Within JDL the chaya was complemented by the "scholar."[10] The scholar formulated JDL Ideology, thereby imbuing the actions of the chaya with a necessity founded in "reason." The scholar was said to "educate" American Jews about their situation and to motivate them to re-

[10] Although I use the terms scholar and chaya throughout this book to represent contrasting ways of becoming JDLers, members of the league employed a variety of additional terms to signify chayas and scholars (e.g., fighter, educator; strong Jews, intellectuals; and so on).

nounce their *galut* personality and behavior. The meaning of the term scholar extended beyond its intra-JDL linkages with the term chaya. Scholar was used to designate the rabbis and teachers of Jewish tradition, and in this connection scholar implied the essence of Judaism. Although the JDL scholar, engaging in the activities of the movement, was not involved in religious lore and education, the use of the word scholar related back to centuries of Jewish scholarship within the religious tradition, thereby infusing the everyday research and ideological dissemination of JDL's scholar with the tones of Judaism's most hallowed traditions. (Chapters four and five discuss the relation, in JDL's version of Jewish History, between the scholarly, religious tradition and the episodes of heroic resistance to anti-Semitism.) In this sense scholar ultimately encompasses chaya: chayas are made "authentic" through their Historic integration with scholars. Theoretically JDLers could justify the chaya as being part of the scholar (the "Jew") in a world of anti-Semitism, but the essence of the Jew (the Jew apart from the hard facts of the real world) remained that of the scholar.

Additionally the term scholar was applied by JDLers to the Jewish "establishment." The relatively large-scale research of, for instance, the Anti-Defamation League and the American Jewish Committee was envied by league members. This research was differentiated from that of JDL's scholars, however, on the basis of the uses to which it was put. JDLers claimed that these organizations gathered piles of potentially valuable data about modern Jewry and about anti-Semitism but that they never used this material to the advantage of the American Jew. A young JDLer asked a group of leaguers, busy collecting information from newspapers and magazines, how their work differed from the activities of the major Jewish groups. She was told:

> We're different from them. Yeah, they have more stuff than us. But they have rooms full of files and they never

open them. We'll use this material. We need it for ideology and for actions and we're going to put a lot of this . . . into pamphlets which people will read.

Although JDLers denigrated the scholarly work of the "establishment" groups, the inclusion of these groups within the category of scholar joined them with JDL and with all Jews in sharing an essential Jewish "predisposition." That the "establishment's" scholarship was seen to misunderstand the situation of the Jew, that scholars without chayas were deemed "useless," even that the scholarship of the "establishment" was viewed to foster belief in the possibility of benevolent "assimilation," a possibility which JDLers denied, all of that did not negate for JDLers their tie, as Jews, with those American Jews whom they openly provoked and disdained.

While aiming to embody the amalgamation of scholar and chaya, JDLers employed the two terms to indicate opposite attributes and tendencies. Each term covered an array of significations in contrast with the significations of the other term. Both terms were remarkably overdetermined in the sense that they contrasted modes of being and becoming *and* suggested a coalescence. The scholar was an educator; the chaya, a fighter. The scholar's role recalled a religious tradition; the chaya's, a fully profane world. The scholar might be a bureaucrat; the chaya, an activist. Scholars were men or women; chayas were men.[11] Scholars worked in offices, at desks; chayas worked in the streets. When scholars acted they always understood why (although scholars were perceived as not acting often enough); chayas sometimes acted without "rationalization" (although this

---

11 Although the chaya squad was not officially closed to females, it was generally agreed that the "work" of the chaya was "work" only males could adequately carry out. One young JDL female did join the squad at one point but did not remain a member for more than a few months. Young women within JDL grumbled about the "male chauvinism" of the league from time to time, but on the whole they accepted a peripheral ("female") position.

was generally devalued). Scholars existed in *galut,* as the glory and tragedy of diaspora Jewry; chayas were rare in the centuries of exile. The scholar geared attention inward toward the education of the Jew; the chaya engaged in confrontation with the non-Jew. Scholars could be "weak"; chayas were above all strong.

The combination of these two sets of tendencies within JDL depended on a balancing of chayas and scholars in such a way that the undesirable aspects of one tendency were obliterated by those of the other tendency. The negative side of the scholar has already been indicated as the inability to act when threatened. The negative side of the chaya was to overact, to act when not threatened, or, more exactly, to act out of concert with the actions of the wider group. Actions carried out by the chaya, taking place in the "street," where the normal rules of social interaction did not hold, gave positive sanction to tolerating chaya's behavior even when it was a "little crazy."

The development of sub-divisions within the league, as the separation of chayas and scholars, faced JDL with the need to underscore the complementarity of the separate tasks and to try to establish a hierarchy for making decisions and seeing that they were enacted. The later need became manifest after Kahane moved to Israel in late 1971 (even during 1971-1972, when he spent every other month in the United States), since most major decisions had previously been referred to and settled by him. Explicit roles and lines of designated authority tended to be either ignored or complied with ambivalently; JDLers saw formal organization as the commencement of a "bureaucracy" that mitigated the distinctions between the league and the "establishment."

During this period the problem of sustaining the spontaneity of the chayas while establishing a system of discipline and authority came to the fore. Ideally the chayas represented the creative energies of the New Jew, in counterdistinction to the vulnerable Jew of the diaspora. Chayas stood for the invigoration of the modern Jew, and were depicted as the *galut* counterpart to Israel itself. Yet, even conceptually, the creation of the chaya depended on interaction with the most extreme Other, the anti-Semite. While epitomizing JDL's internality, the actualization of the chaya occurred at the limits of JDL's external world. Indeed, the word chaya implied the life of the wilds, the undomesticated animal. The practical dilemma of maintaining discipline within the squad was paralleled by the conceptual effort to retain the character of the inside while acting on the margins of the outside.[12] After a breach of discipline within the squad a JDL leader spoke to the chayas, saying: "It's sick if you look forward to going out to fight . . . originally the chayas were picked because they were better . . . but I have a nightmare about the chaya squad becoming a goon squad."

JDL unanimously perceived actual transformations of the chaya squad into a "goon squad" as a jeopardous possibility, to be avoided at all costs. Yet JDLers often described themselves in terms suggesting some of the connotations of a

---

[12] This situation presents similarities to the marginal quality of certain types of ritual. Mary Douglas (1966), analyzing the powerful correlates of disorder, recalls Radcliffe-Brown's description of the Andaman Islander who "leaves his band and wanders into the forest like a madman. When he returns to his senses and to human society he has gained occult power of healing . . ." (1966:114). Similarly, the chaya in the margins of the city was seen as a "healer" of the disease, anti-Semitism. Analogies between the chaya and the healer or doctor were made by JDLers; one of these placed the chaya as analogous to the surgeon, with anti-Semitism analogous to a cancer that had to be removed surgically, i.e., through direct physical excision. There are obviously major differences between the healing abilities of the lone Andaman wanderer and those developed in the group effort of the chaya squad, and I am not proposing that existence in the sociocultural margins actually produces the ability to "heal." I only want to indicate the parallel metaphors within two widely different cultures. It is additionally suggestive that marginal frontiers of urban society are likely to be placed at the geographical center of that very society. The "wild" and the "undomesticated" are not envisioned far off beyond the village but near the heart of the city.

goon squad. Such descriptions did not always condemn. For instance, the use of the English word "animal" was sometimes applied favorably by JDLers to themselves, although this same term was used with the utmost derision in labeling individuals or groups deemed to be anti-Semitic.[13] And the image of a goon squad was seen by many JDL critics, especially from within the Jewish community, as the reality of JDL. JDLers responded to such repudiations by renouncing the life-style of American Jews as a perversion of "authentic" Judaism. Anti-JDL Jews could condemn JDL and call for its disbanding, but JDLers included all Jews as potentially part of their movement as recipients of JDL "defense." According to JDLers, even those Jews most resistant to supporting the league benefited from the changed image of the American Jew that the league effected. Speaking at a meeting of JDL youth in Brooklyn in January 1972, one of the movement's leaders said, "Now when a car is stopped and the riders are wearing yarmulkas, it is searched for guns. That is a nice thing." As an image projected to non-Jews, the more extreme the chaya appeared, the better. The danger was that images, not made *ex nihilo*, but in action, could irremediably encompass essential identity.

Now that we have seen what the basic terms of JDL identity are, we can consider a nuclear series of alternative options for integrating scholar and chaya within the league. JDLers have appropriated three options offered by an individualistic "universe" for identifying themselves vis-à-vis

[13] Specific animal names were sometimes employed in referring to weak diaspora Jews as well as to anti-Semites and themselves. When applied to diaspora Jewry, animal names (e.g., "lemmings," "jellyfish") suggested the absence of strength and the lack of ability or intentions necessary for self-defense. When anti-Semites were labeled "animals" (the generic term animal was generally used in reference to anti-Semites rather than particular species), the label implied a lack of "reason." (Cf., Fernandez 1972 on animal names as metaphors and Leach 1964.)

each other and the wider society (see Barnett 1973a, 1973b, n.d.; Dumont 1965a, 1965b, 1970; MacPherson 1962). There was general agreement that ideally each individual JDLer should be both chaya and scholar, both fighter and educator, able to operate in the street and in the sanctuary, to confront the Other and to inform the Self. The ideal locus of value, in short, was the individual person. There was equal agreement, however, that this ideal was probably unattainable within the context of the league. The paucity of individual scholar-chayas was often pointed out as the primary cause of the movement's internal difficulties and of the failure of specific demonstrations, actions, and league projects. The following remark of one active JDLer typifies this concern: "The trouble with JDL is a division between scholars and chayas with very few people being both." Before Kahane moved to Israel and even during those months in 1971-1972 when he was in the U. S., it was easier to sustain the valorization of the individual person, for Kahane mediated the scholars and chayas, convinced each of the need for the other, and drew them together.

During 1971 an alternative stress began to emerge. The level of integration within the movement started to shift from one of equivalent individuals acting similarly and in unison to different sorts of people whose dissimilar activities could be combined and instigated at the level of the collectivity. JDL as a whole, rather than the individual JDLer, became the unit within which chaya and scholar had to be made to co-exist harmoniously. Chaya and scholar remained mutually exclusive individuals, in fact, but as symbols they had to be combined; the combination locus became JDL. This adjustment far from obliterated the importance of the individual JDLer, who became ever the more necessary since less fully replicated by every other JDLer. Though individuals may have been more necessary, they could not stand alone, as qualitatively sufficient. The increasing stress on the group as the locus of value was part and parcel of JDL's attempts to maintain internal cohesion in the absence of

Kahane. The movement as a whole was posited as a conceptual reproduction of the man.

That shift, the basis for the symbolic construct discussed in the next section, was never fully actualized. When Kahane moved to Israel, the league also began to emphasize the importance of *aliyah* (immigration to Israel). Just when JDLers in the U. S. were beginning to develop alternative modes of integration in Kahane's absence, they were presented with a new form of individualism—the relation between individual person and nation. (This relation is discussed in chapter four.) Thus the years 1971-1972 were particularly trying for American JDLers, who were torn between three alternative individualistic perspectives, one of which meant the dissolution of an American JDL. Of the other two alternatives, one entailed the valorization of the individual within JDL and the other, the valorization of the whole; the first, almost by definition, could not achieve integration without Kahane, and in practice, I would suggest, neither could the second.

Even when chaya and scholar were taken as two desired components, each necessary and together sufficient for the existence of JDL, the particular form of the relation was still at issue since the same queries could be raised about scholars and chayas from the vantage point of the collectivity as from that of the individual JDL member: Within JDL should scholars encompass chayas or vice versa? Do the two indicate equivalent though distinct sorts of behavior? Are they incomparable as concepts? Or as behaviors? These questions are not simply permutations but actual suggestions of JDLers. Such questions encapsulate JDLers' struggle toward self-definition, although the questions were not explicitly enumerated. In 1971-1972 JDLers were struggling toward a self-conception in terms of the valorized collectivity, but the struggle was confounded by the earlier valorization of the individual and by the growing involvement in advocating *aliyah* as well as by increasing numbers of JDLers actually moving to Israel.

Within the league active members found themselves more often identified as either scholar or chaya, although in relation to non-JDL Jews, all saw themselves as chayas, and in relation to non-Jews, as scholars. The "youth," who spent more time each day than the adults in league activities, and from whom members of the chaya squad tended to be drawn, gave greater significance to the choice of identifying as scholar or chaya. There was not always a close correlation between self-identification as chaya or scholar and an individual's being categorized similarly by other JDLers. In general, however, the leaguer who identified in one way or the other was so viewed by others. There did exist a fairly distinct split in attitudes toward the nature of the scholar and the chaya and toward their desired integration: scholars emphasized the equivalence of the two, and chayas de-emphasized this equivalence in favor of either an encompassing of the scholar or a declaration of noncomparability between the two categories. As mentioned previously, the perceived danger of the chayas' encompassing the scholars was the elimination of that essence that unified JDL with the wider Jewish community—past, present, and future.

We can see the dimensions of the preferred relation between chaya and scholar by looking at several instances of deliberation and conflict among JDLers concerning the relation. A long and heated conversation between an eighteen-year-old JDLer who considered herself a scholar and a seventeen-year-old member of the chaya squad exemplifies these differences in perspective. The discussion concerned the future of the league and the sorts of priorities that were to be selected in organizing the activities of the coming year. I shall call the two parties to the conversation Susan and Henry, although these are not their real names. While this argument does represent the areas of dispute, it must be noted that the positions expressed on both sides are extreme, correlating with Henry's total identification as a chaya and Susan's unusually intense convictions about the need for what she called "education" within the movement.

Susan argued that the league needed scholars as much as chayas and that, while the "work" of the chaya was necessary in dealing with immediate anti-Semitism, the task of educating American Jewry about the exigency of militant reaction in the U. S. and of *aliyah*, given existing anti-Semitism, was in the long run of equal, if not primary, importance. "We need educators and scholars," she asserted. "If we don't save our souls, then how can we save our bodies in the end either?" Henry regarded this as missing the point of JDL. "Chayas," he contended, "*are* JDL." Later in the discussion he said, "Other Jews might not see this, but we're saving their bodies. We're breaking our asses because of them. Maybe it's because you're new to JDL. Don't you see, JDL is fighters. Education isn't even a tenth best." The tone of the conversation became increasingly strained; the necessity and value of the chaya was questioned, however, by neither Henry nor Susan. Eventually Susan, while not capitulating, began to mitigate her own position by underscoring her possible marginality as a relatively new member of JDL. Susan's concession has ramifications beyond determinations of the length of time it takes to become a socialized JDLer. Although she had only been an active member of JDL for a few months when this conversation took place, the positions she endorsed were recognized by all JDLers and approved by many. The marginality that both Susan and Henry attributed to Susan is a commentary on the position of scholars within the league, much more than on Susan's lack of familiarity with JDL.

Paradoxically, JDL was marginal within American Jewry because of the chaya—neither JDL, nor "establishment" Jews, nor public media disputed this, although that marginality was obviously construed differently by each—but within JDL, the scholar, who incorporated the league's assertion of being essentially Jewish, was marginal. The scholar within JDL was in the ambiguous position of countenancing, indeed ostensibly conceiving and expressing, the movement's Ideology while at the same time symbolizing within JDL certain behaviors associated by leaguers with their image of the non-JDL American Jew. JDL "action" was presaged and justified in Ideology, but the Ideologue (the scholar) was perceived as reticent when it was really time to act. The fact that one of the primary functions of the scholar was the presentation and dissemination of JDL Ideology is vital in understanding the nature of the scholar's ambiguous position. That function was almost exclusively in Kahane's hands before he moved to Israel; practically all of JDL's original Ideological statements were formulated by him. In his absence the task of continuing that responsibility was given to designated sub-divisions of JDLers (the scholars). Kahane described the existence of a league Ideology as imperative in integrating the movement internally, for it was Ideology that instructed the chaya about when to fight and when not to, and it was Ideology that informed the non-chaya (and non-JDL Jew) about the need for physical strength.

JDL Ideology as a symbol becomes an alternative metaphor for the valorization of the collective whole. When Kahane handled the creation of Ideology, chayas within JDL saw the Ideology in this way. But Kahane, and Kahane alone, was able to persuade the chayas that comprehension of and adherence to the movement's Ideology was a necessary part of their task as chayas. As he stood for JDL, so the Ideology stood for him. With Kahane in Israel, JDL chayas increasingly defined themselves as individual "Jewish fighters," capable of carrying out their "work" without the "educators" and "philosophers." The valorization of JDL as a collectivity grew almost entirely from the scholar half of the league. That valorization was accepted by chayas only to the extent that they identified with the larger movement and accepted the significance of a movement Ideology.

The conversation between Susan and Henry, indicating discrepant perspectives of and toward scholars and chayas, entertains variant approaches to the two intersecting domains. The first is the arena of identity/image and the second that of autonomy/heteronomy (Marcuse 1972). The identity/image contrast bears primary significance to construction of internality *and* externality, at the level of JDL versus other Jews, and at the level of Jews versus non-Jews. The autonomy/heteronomy contrast was invoked internally in constructing the scholar and chaya *within* the league. With the valorization of the collectivity, symbolic heteronomy enveloped the autonomy of the individual JDLer who, reproducing *part of* the whole, was entitled to join in the autonomous freedom *of the group*. The shift toward collective stress, condoning internal heteronomy, within which each individual participated, depended on a balancing of scholar and chaya. Without that balance, JDL was faced with heteronomy *ordained externally,* faced, that is, with the loss of illusions of freedom. Had the chaya attained internal authority, the risk was the attenuation of Judaic authenticity. The conceptual struggle to balance the chaya and the scholar relied on the incorporation of the chaya within the essence of Judaism, through the model of Historic Jews as people of *action*, and on the maintenance of a movement Ideology, presuming to embody Judaic "values" in advocating the physical defense of Jewry. Finally, however, the chaya was worthless without the attendant image, the image of invincible strength and undaunted courage. And, the image of the chaya could no more be balanced with the identity of the scholar than can the Apollonian be balanced with the Dionysian: the result would be Apollonian.

Metaphors about the league as analogous to a "family" are suggestive. The call to action in the name of "your brothers and sisters" was a frequent JDL refrain. "JDL," said one leaguer, "is like a large, large family." Following Schneider's analysis, the family in America "resolves the radical opposition between nature and human reason" (1968:37). For JDL, the scholar, representing the "natural" Jewish "predisposition," was the epitome of human reason. That reason was deemed to have been fulfilled *within* the

Jewish communities and between Jews and sacred scripture but to have failed in comprehending the relation between Jew and non-Jew, and/or, given comprehension, in acting to defend the Jew. Among Jews therefore chayas were viewed as products of culture, the cultural counterpart to Jewish reason in a universe of non-Jews. The equivalent of the chaya among non-Jews ("goon") was placed by JDLers in the realm of nature. Within the "family" (JDL) the nature of the Jew combined with the nature of the non-Jew, but that second nature had to undergo a conceptual transformation to become the culture of the Jew, necessary in a world of non-Jews. JDL scholars were natural and rational; chayas were the product of that rationality, but not always themselves rational.

One JDLer's metaphor, likening the league to a family, contains in striking form the contradictions and an attempted resolution. This leaguer was speaking to a group of JDL members about the need for participation in a newly conceived JDL project. "You will be working," he said, "with your brothers and sisters, and I emphasize brother and sister. . . . There is a definite feeling of kinship with the problem and this work is very important." The words "kinship with the problem" suggest not only that the problem of any Jew is the problem of every Jew, but that the problem itself is part of the metaphoric family. The existence of the anti-Semite (or "goon") gave the symbolic inducement, "rationalizing" (naturalizing or making "Jewish") the indispensability of chayas (JDL). Ideally, the chayas were like "goons" only in the dimension of strength; the difference was envisioned as that between the irrational action of hoodlums, fighting because they enjoy it, and the well-thought action of Jewish heroes, fighting from necessity.

Scholars and chayas alike accepted and worked to achieve that opposition; equaling or surpassing the anti-Semite in strength, the chaya had to substantiate the "reason" defining the chaya as "Jew." In the street, however, the chaya was dealing with the "problem" of anti-Semitism *and* constituting personal identity. The chaya left the "office" (the "home" of JDL) to protect the largest "family" of Jews, and in the street the disorder of physical confrontation paralleled a potential disorder in categorization. The street could legitimate chayas or transform them so that they would become out of place at "home." An elderly JDLer, reprimanding a group of rambunctious chayas in the league office, advised, "Just because you're a chaya on the street doesn't mean you have to be a chaya in the office as well." This was said quasi-humorously; the chastizing intent of the remark was mitigated by its complimentary innuendo that one can hardly be too much a chaya. But alongside that second sentiment stood an apprehension about the possibility of the chaya's having been changed into a "goon," the objectionable transformation of chaya.

Within the office, the particular domain of the JDL scholar, the collective whole was the locus of value and the source of authority. The dictates of league ideology (the "philosophical" representation of the whole) empowered the chaya to go into the street, but once there, the locus of value shifted. In the street the individual "Jewish fighter" was expected to be disciplined in obedience to the leaders of the squad, and in opposition to the "anti-Semite." Those squad leaders, selected to fight well *and* to comprehend JDL ideology, were entrusted with precluding the possibility of "irrational" action. Rationality was defined internally; in the street the chaya had to enact the axioms of reason through the medium of physical confrontation. Increasingly, strict discipline within the squad was demanded as an antidote to the observation that "the best fighters . . . aren't always the best thinkers."

The chayas' relation to the larger group and to JDL "reason" was tested in 1972 when a group of chayas planned an action against a self-proclaimed Nazi. This person, a student at a university in New York, had brandished a flag with a swastika on it in his dormitory window and had publicly espoused Nazi beliefs. Kahane was in the U. S. at the time and was scheduled to speak at the university that week. The chayas intended to put on a "show" of their own. At a meeting to outline their scheme of action, the chayas made a point of the reasonableness of their plans. Several persons noted that Kahane might not approve of their activities, but all agreed that they would continue with their plans whether or not the "Reb" gave his consent. These JDLers thought there might be "trouble" during Kahane's speech, and saw their role as protecting him. "The Reb," said one leaguer, "is incredible. Normally, if a guy is talking and there's trouble in the audience, he steps back. Not the Reb. He jumps down every time." When the JDLers got to the university, they met Kahane on their way in. He told them in no uncertain terms to "go home" with the admonition that their behavior was "really irrational." Kahane stopped the group from proceeding with their plans, telling them, "It's necessary to think about things like this before you do them. You can't plan actions on your own. . . . We're a large movement. . . . You'll only hurt us. This is not the right time or place. . . . Do you want to hurt the Jewish people?" When the JDLers involved agreed not to go ahead with their plans, they did not deliberate the rationality or irrationality of these plans. Their decision was phrased in terms of authority. Rather than continuing to justify the reasonableness of their contemplated activities, they concluded that rational or irrational, "we can't go against the Reb."

In the speech Kahane proceeded to give, he disagreed with the way the students and administration of the university had handled the display of the swastika. Neo-Nazis, he suggested, should be physically assaulted and should certainly not be allowed freedom to express fascist belief. After listening to this speech several of the JDLers whom Kahane had earlier reprimanded noted an apparent discrepancy between Kahane's having stopped them and his advocacy of physical confrontation. They did not, however, see this as a contradiction. In the words of one of them, "The Reb can think. . . . He knows when to fight. . . . It would have been a bad image if we went in there with helmets . . . and stuff. . . . The Reb sure told them. He really is JDL." *Through Kahane*, personal autonomy survives the fact of "obedience."

In the above episode, "image" emerged as a product of internal "discipline" controlling physical "strength." The chaya was prevented from becoming a "goon" through discipline, and the illusion of autonomy was retained through the individual's ability to identify as part of the authority. In Kahane's absence the Ideological authorities (scholars) leaned, in the eyes of the chaya, toward sacrificing strength, and the image makers (chayas) leaned, in the eyes of the scholars, toward undermining collective autonomy through unfettered individual strength.

A demonstration in the winter of 1972 that did not achieve its aims was pointed to by JDLers as an example of the undesirable consequences of the scholar's relative timidity with regard to physical confrontation. Two leaguers, both about eleven years old, returned to the JDL office with the story that a group of chayas had run rather than fight. When the chayas returned they were faced with this account and tried to deny it somewhat and to excuse it otherwise by blaming a particular JDL leader, whom they saw as a scholar, for curtailing their freedom to act as they had wanted. A JDL leader ("Michael") had remained in the office during the demonstration and was placed in the role of arbitrator by the returning demonstrators. Michael listened to the accounts amidst rising commotion, reiterating several times, "Just one thing. Did our people run?" When it became obvious that a coherent story was not going to emerge in the immediate confusion, Michael stopped the discussion, declaring, "We'll find out if our chayas ran. That can't be tolerated. Too many educators around here . . . there is no excuse for this kind of thing. Never again, I tell you, never again." The use of "never again" brought home the similarity between the demonstrators' behavior and JDL's characterization of diaspora Jewry as cowardly.

While disciplined chayas without strength weakened JDL's image, strong chayas without discipline suggested a breakdown in internal cohesion. At a meeting of JDL women[14] the subject of chaya "misbehavior" was broached in connection with plans for housing JDLers scheduled to go to a league demonstration in a distant city. One woman suggested, "We should train our chayas to be polite." When a second woman protested that this was impossible since "the chayas are really animals," general altercation broke out among the women. One might ask: What does it mean to be really an animal as opposed to really a chaya, remembering that chaya means animal in Hebrew? And then note: the fact that people can really be chayas went undisputed. At issue was the statement that "chayas are really animals."

Discipline was seen as necessary in preventing image (strength) from absorbing identity, but the locus of value, the authority for discipline, had to be placed in such a way that it did not appear to eclipse the sense of autonomy. JDLers stipulated that self-discipline was absolutely necessary for collective unity and thus for substantialized rationality. The vital step emerged in JDLers' postulations about the most effective source for the development of self-

---

[14] JDL's "women's group," one of the several sub-groups to develop in the early 1970s, held fairly regular meetings at the Brooklyn headquarters, and was composed for the most part of married, middle-aged women who explicitly relegated their activities to "female projects." In notifying JDLers of the formation of the women's group, the *Jewish Defense League Newsletter* read:

> For many months we have been trying to form a separate, active women's group. There are many obvious reasons for this, reasons that compel every major national group to do the same thing. The women will, of course, remain regular members of the JDL and will participate in regular JDL meetings with the men (*Jewish Defense League Newsletter*, Vol. 1 (4), January 9, 1970).

discipline. From compliance with the laws of the religious Jew, from obedience to *kashrut* (laws concerning ritual fitness of food) and to the conventions of *shabbot* (sabbath) and ritual purity, came the securest path, said JDLers, toward personal discipline. "Kashrut," explained one JDL leader "is totally a spiritual concept . . . it is a guide to rational living. . . . The purpose is to discipline you, to give you strength." Although the leaguer who said this is an Orthodox Jew, similar premises were upheld by many non-religious JDLers who saw religious observance as a metaphor for, if not the reality of, self-discipline. Kahane, emphasizing the value of kashrut writes:

> If the beast of the field is driven by his biological needs, man must master them and harness them. . . . The Jew who waits an extra hour or two because he is unable to find kosher food near his place of work . . . is a Jew who is strong, disciplined and the master of his "I" (1971:205).

Whether the equivalence between self-discipline demanded within JDL and that ordained by the laws of Orthodoxy was taken literally or analogically the effect placed the most criticized activities of the league within the domain of the sacred. The strength and discipline of the movement, and of the chaya, became another working out of processes defined as fundamentally Jewish. Kahane's reference in the quoted sentences on kashrut, to the "beast of the field" (or goon) can be likened to the undisciplined chaya, whose very name means animal. The realization of these similarities could be precluded by the imputation of a religious Judaism into the foundations of the chaya's behavior. The form in which individual JDLers were organized into the collectivity signified the integration of the league with the most sacred aspects of Judaism.

By combining individual self-discipline, as the building block of collective valorization, with the essence of Judaism, an image was conjoined with identity and the illusion of

autonomy was retained—but only the illusion, for to quote
Marcuse, discussing a different religious tradition:

> . . . this anti-authoritarian tendency is only the comple-
> ment of an order which is directly tied to the functioning
> of as yet opaque relations of authority. From the very
> outset the bourgeois concept of freedom left the way open
> for the recognition of certain metaphysical authorities
> and this recognition permits external unfreedom to be
> perpetuated within the human soul (1972:54).

In enacting the scholar and the chaya a series of paradoxes ensued; many of them were dealt with on an ad hoc
basis. Ultimately the paradoxes re-emerged. But what was
the symbolic construct through which JDLers related their
movement to the relevant Others of their social present
(1971-1972)? The construct was an attempt to mediate the
contradictions, and although left unarticulated in JDL
Ideology, it was the tacit model for (and of) a pattern of
strategies that the league adopted. Once the construct is
presented, I shall show with two illustrations how it, too,
failed.

By being chaya and scholar the JDL partook of qualities
attributed to the "establishment" Jew (or, generalizing, to
the non-JDL Jew) and qualities attributed to the non-Jew
(even to the anti-Semite). But by the same account JDLers
attempted to demarcate themselves as scholars compared to
chayas and as chayas compared to scholars. The following
precepts are suggested:

> a) chaya (Historic heroes):scholar :: JDL:non-JDL Jews
> b) chaya ("goon"):scholar :: non-Jews:JDL

JDL and JDL alone stands between Jews and non-Jews.
This was not seen as a defaulting on the movement's allegation of being quintessentially Jewish, since the non-JDL
Jews to whom JDLers contrasted themselves were defined
precisely through not being fully authentic in their Juda-

ism. Rather, JDLers could see their group as the only group adequate to be a Jewish mediator in a non-Jewish world. In practice, maintaining the symbolic separation between Jew and non-Jew was guaranteed only through interaction across the boundary, and in that interaction the boundary became a bridge. JDL was a tricky mediator, however, presuming to span the extremes of the social present in action and simultaneously to adumbrate a genuine and temporally non-contextualized Judaism.

First, a strategic scenario envisioned by JDL and relying on the concretizing of the first precept will be considered. The intention of this scenario was to effect the successful negotiation of particular demands, viewed as beneficial to American Jews in general, with the relevant authority—often the government. The strategy: chayas and scholars go together and present their requests. From the start the chayas act "like militants." After a time the chayas storm out, leaving the scholars to negotiate, with the threat that if their somewhat modified demands are not met, the chayas, "who are obviously crazy," might return. JDL suggested to various "establishment" Jewish organizations that they play the scholar to JDL's chaya in the enactment of this plan; the offer of cooperation was refused. Although JDLers presumed this scheme would be maximally auspicious if carried out with a "respected" Jewish group, the tactic was not doomed by the "establishment's" unwillingness to participate. JDL, while chaya to the scholar was also scholar to the chaya, and the movement thereby could undertake such a strategy with JDLers acting the roles of *both* chaya and scholar. Without the JDL other Jews could not do this, even if they wanted to, insofar as, JDLers deemed, non-JDL Jews would not have been able to act like chayas.

The tactic was employed several times. Much to the surprise of the participants, the institution or agency to which the demands were posted never seemed particularly interested in the scholars. "It's the chayas they care about," said one young JDL scholar, after having taken part in such an "action." "They weren't at all impressed by what the scholars did. Who cares about one more Jewish group?" The symbolic construct, placing JDL as a mediator between Jews and non-Jews, was not necessarily destroyed by the failure of the strategy. Symbolic constructs can be held aside in the face of disconfirming evidence or patched up here and there, but the failure of this strategy is indicative of the difficulties that emerged when the construct was tested in action. The tactic qua tactic was *not* an exclusive model of JDL internality but an easily substitutable form of political action available to any group, and could not be used to win the case at hand *and* prove authentic Jewishness in one act.

Failure in the working of the first precept of the construct defining the mediator (JDL) was not as serious for the league as failure in the working of the second precept. The differences between JDL and "anti-Semites" (and goons) were of paramount significance; if this went, the Self-Other boundary would have been on the verge of collapse. A decision made by JDL in 1972 (though never, in fact, effected) reflects the second of the two precepts and points to a real breakdown in self-identification. It was felt at that time that the number of people in the actual chaya squad should be increased. When it appeared that there were not enough members of the JDL who could become active chaya squad members, the league resolved to use newspaper advertising in the quest for potential chaya squad members among non-JDLers. The chance to join the squad was to be extended not only to non-JDL Jews but to non-Jews as well.[15] In this way the symbolic equivalence between JDL and non-Jews, when compared with relevant aspects of non-JDL Jews, becomes a concrete amalgamation. But it is an amalgamation seeming to swallow up the symbolic construct within which it was supposed to occur and which it was supposed to reflect. The decision to open the

[15] The people who joined the chaya squad on this basis were to be given full membership in the squad, but they were not thereby to be given automatic membership in JDL.

squad to non-Jews resulted partly from the lack of success encountered with strategies like that described above. "If we can't be successful scholars," went the rationale, "then let's be better chayas." Yet the admitting of non-Jewish chayas into the squad would have entailed the possibility that scholars might have been absolutely encompassed by chayas and, more drastically, Jews by non-Jews.

JDL related itself to non-JDLers at the level of the collective whole. The symbolic construct through which the movement saw itself mediating these Others was paralleled at the intra-movement level. Here, however, the intent to mediate opposing types (scholars and chayas) was not mitigated, and finally nullified, by the Ideological importance of maintaining a well-defined separation at the same time. Like JDL at the collective level, those rare individuals within the movement who combined within themselves the "fighter" and the "educator" could mediate scholars and chayas by being both. Kahane, the unquestioned leader of the movement, was seen to best, in fact alone, exemplify this union. Kahane was metaphorically JDL.

Sartre, dealing with an individual's part in concrete historic episodes writes:

> Through the individual the group looks back to itself and finds itself again in the particular opaqueness of life as well as in the universality of its struggle. Or rather, this universality takes on the face, the body, and the voice of the leaders whom it has given to itself (1963:130).

A handwritten sign, which hung for many months on the walls of the JDL Identity Center in Brooklyn, read: "Meir Kahane cannot be silenced for we are all Meir Kahane." Kahane became the symbol of a unified JDL, and that symbolism transcended its failures. At a moment of discord among several JDL leaders, one of them turned to the sign and said, "Sometimes I think it's the other way around. JDL cannot be silenced only because Meir is JDL." A leader's "irreducible particularity," writes Sartre, "is one way of living universality" (1963:130).

CHAPTER IV

Upright Kneeling

"WHAT thus seems to take place outside ideology . . . in reality takes place in ideology. What really takes place in ideology seems therefore to take place outside it. That is why those who are in ideology believe themselves by definition outside ideology . . ." (Althusser 1971:163). In these words Louis Althusser is implicating the most normal, mundane, and unquestioned aspects of daily life as ideological. Just when ideology seems farthest afield—as when, following Althusser's example, one responds to a greeting in the street—one is reacting from and within ideology. Those actions and beliefs that appear especially natural or typical may illustrate most strikingly the form in which the individual is grasped by and is grasping ideological representations. If not, however, by living a *particular* ideology ("world outlook") "we admit that the ideology we are discussing from a critical point of view, examining it as the ethnologist examines the myths of a 'primitive society,' that these 'world outlooks' are largely imaginary, i.e., do not 'correspond to reality' " (Althusser 1971:153).

JDL formalized an Ideology, presented in pamphlets and expressed publicly as *the* league stance. JDLers learned this Ideology by reading these publications, listening to Kahane's speeches, and attending seminars. All JDLers were highly conscious of the Ideology *as an ideology* and saw it to be the most adequate definition of the league's achievements and "aims." Systematization of a JDL Ideology commenced in the first months of the league's existence and by 1972 had gone through three stages. Ideological stress shifted from (a) a short early period when emphasis was given to the league's exemplification and defense of the

"American dream" to (b) ordination of a JDL "philosophy," accenting correspondence with and insertion in Jewish History and Judaic universalism to (c) incorporation of *aliyah* as an Ideological obligation with stress on settlement in Israel as the only "reasonable" response given anti-Semitism and as a religious mandate prescribed by Orthodox Judaism. These shifts in stress clearly correlate with the variation in stress from valorization of the individual person to valorization of the collective whole to valorization of the individual vis-à-vis the "nation" (Israel). In the first place, the individual JDLer represents the pluperfect American, who in this case happens to be a Jew and who seeks a rightful due within the American "system." In the second place, the movement as a whole encapsulates itself as an American ethnic group with particular Jewish needs and concerns. In the third place, ethnicity is transposed into nationalism under the dictum that Jewish needs and concerns cannot be met in a non-Jewish land. JDL's Ideological statements in stages (b) and (c), respectively, differ formally only in the addition of nationalism in the second case. That nationalism, which became increasingly the focus of league Ideology, combined the necessity of "defense" (in this case through emigration) against anti-Semitism with the language of religious authority. Orthodox Judaism does ordain that the Jew, if able, should live in *eretz Yisroel* (the land of Israel).

JDL's leaders envisioned the future of the movement as dependent on the public availability and reception of the movement's Ideology. Ideology channeled behavior by providing conceptual guidelines and instilled action with meaning through authorization by the highest concerns. That which was done in the name of Ideology was a priori justified, since it was conceptually insertable within Historic thought and action. The most direct model for league Ideology was the revisionist movement of Vladimir Jabotinsky. That movement, which gave birth to Betar, the Irgun, and Israel's Herut Party, was seen as the most recent

link in the "chain" of Jewish heroes. To demonstrate similarity with revisionism was simultaneously and by "definition" to prove similarity with ancient heroes. Given that
identification, the next step enabled proof of Historic
authenticity in action to rest on concordance between action
and JDL Ideology, itself. This was possible because JDLers,
although "committed" to the movement's Ideology, consciously stood outside that Ideology. The league Ideology
did provide representations of the world, and those representations were taken up by members, but in addition,
Ideology as a whole was reified as a symbol of the league,
and Ideological reception symbolized the individual's
choosing to be a JDLer.

Several aspects of ideology must be distinguished. As
noted above, systematized JDL ideology is denoted as
Ideology. The phenomenological appropriation of that
Ideology by the individual JDLer will be denoted as
"ideology." By ideology, I denote the common-sense beliefs
and practices that JDLers share because they are modern
Americans. That is, ideology is the "natural" and taken-for-
granted, and is therefore not the object of self-conscious
reflection; it grounds the "real" (cf., Barnett n.d.). Actions
and representations sustaining the individual's *belief* that
s/he was acting and thinking in tune with JDL Ideology
are "ideological." "Ideology" and Ideology play off one
another; "ideology" is more concrete, more malleable, and
less universalistic in its pretensions. "Ideology" is anchored
in Ideology, not because Ideology holds "ideology" still, but
because the "veracity" of Ideology is used as a base against
which to dispute, deny, justify, or prove "ideology." JDLers
think they are inside "ideology" but they are really outside
—in ideology. "Ideology" provides the ground for the dialectic between Ideology and ideology, which is a permutation of American ideology; here, JDLers believe they are
outside while being inside.

The notational forms for ideology parallel those for history. This parallel is more than grammatical. Ideology and History empower "ideology" and "history," and the context in which they are empowered is ideological and historical. Althusser analyzes Christian religious ideology, in illustrating the form of ideology in general as a relation of "subjection" between subjects (individuals) and their Subject ("unique" and "absolute"). In (this) ideology, writes Althusser, one is "a subject through the Subject subjected to the Subject" (1971:167; in italics in original). Similarly for JDL: ideology is "ideologized" in the name of Ideology, and history is "historicized" in the name of History; "ideologization" and "historicization" are the processes of subjection.

This chapter and the next deal with the process through which Ideology becomes "ideology" (i.e., believed to be true) and the relation between that process and ideology (that process *is* ideological). This chapter considers the connection between JDL "actions" (e.g., demonstrations) and JDL Ideology/"ideology" within the American context, and implications of the incorporation of nationalism into JDL Ideology. The next chapter focuses on the ideological relation between Self (JDL, Jew) and Other ("political extremist," WASP, black, Italian and so on) in the United States.

First, in order to examine the Jewish Defense League Ideology in some detail, the following exposition sticks as closely as possible to the formal Ideology as it appears in pamphlets and booklets printed by JDL[1] but also uses some material from seminars and public speeches when clarification is necessary. (Pieces of some of this material appeared in the previous chapters.) What I am about to present is the version of JDL Ideology that was first syste-

---

[1] JDL publications setting forth the movement's Ideology include: "A Manifesto," "Jewish Defense League: Principles and Philosophy," "Jewish Defense League Youth Handbook," "Jewish Defense League: Youth Movement Handbook," "Three Most Asked Questions of the Jewish Defense League," "Jew Go Home."

matized in late 1969, plus nationalist aspects that were added in late 1971; this Ideology is formalized around the following "five principles":[2]

(a) *Ahavat Yisroel* ("love of Jewry")

It is the duty and the right of each Jew to "love" all fellow Jews, and to feel their "pains" and to participate in their "joys." "All Jews are part of the great body Israel. We are all brothers, we are all sisters, and the love of a brother to a brother and to a sister is the love of one Jew to another" (p. 4). Just as one's first obligation is to one's family, so, also, it is to one's people. Love of another Jew means understanding that person's problems, even sometimes before he does, and acting to help him in his difficulties. An understanding of *ahavat Yisroel* can be gained through studying its absence, through studying the lack of reaction of world Jewish leadership to the holocaust, to the problems of the Soviet Jew, to the "crisis conditions" existing in the U. S. "for Jewish merchants, teachers and civil servants, for Jewish neighborhoods threatened with crime and terror. . . . One struggles to find the same zeal for the Jew as they manifest for others" (p. 6). The "Jewish organizations and Federations" do not express *ahavat Yisroel* when they support "non-Jewish causes," ignoring the poor, oppressed Jew. "Jewish problems . . . must come first for the Jew just as, rightfully, the black problem must come first for the black, or the Irish problem for the Irishman" (pp. 6-7). For a Jew to ignore de jure *or* de facto anti-Semitism is to ignore *ahavat Yisroel*. "The trouble is that our Jewish

[2] This presentation of Jewish Defense League Ideology is not directly quoted from any one source but does represent the tone and meaning of the Ideology. Unless otherwise indicated, all direct quotations are from "Jewish Defense League: Movement Handbook" (not dated but made available to the membership in autumn 1972). Except for the addition of nationalism and some alterations in the presentation of the movement's formal organization, this handbook is identical to "Jewish Defense League: Youth Movement Handbook," made available about a year earlier.

leaders are assimilated Jews. Jews who have lost touch with the common Jew" (p. 7). *Ahavat Yisroel* is linked closely with settlement in the land of Israel and with "a deep respect for the traditions of Israel" (p. 8).

(b) *Hadar* ("dignity and pride")

It was *hadar* "which the great Jewish Leader Zev[3] Jabotinsky attempted to instill in the oppressed and degraded masses of Eastern Europe . . ." (p. 8). It includes pride in being a Jew, in the history and the Torah, in the tragedies and the transcendence of those tragedies. *Hadar* is a response to anti-Semitism, which robs the Jews of first their honor and then their very being. Jews should not be so "sensitive" and so delicate when someone calls them "kikes." Preservation of Jewish honor is a pragmatic duty, ensuring survival and a sacred duty since the honor of the Jewish people is a holy honor. "This call to holiness, the seal of the Jew, is that in which we take pride . . ." (p. 9). Lack of *hadar* is evident in the young diaspora Jew who takes heroes from all sorts of non-Jewish causes, and this lack is evident in his parents who have substituted an "American synthetic version" of Judaism, consisting of food, hotels, and lavish Bar Mitzvahs for authentic, true Judaism. For the JDLer there is *hadar* in being among "those who understand and perceive the reality of Jewish life" (p. 11). That pride must become part of each JDL member's everyday behavior, "in the way he speaks, softly and courteously; in the way he walks, proudly yet not arrogantly; in the respect which he demands from others and which he gives to them" (p. 11).

(c) *Barzel* ("iron")

Barzel, the hallmark of the ancient Jew, of Abraham, Moses, Saul, and David, is a "revolutionary" idea for the *galut* (exiled) Jew. Images of the Jewish weakling must be reversed; the Jews must learn that when they run, they abet the anti-Semite who assumes the next Jew will not fight

[3] "Zev" was the Hebrew name of Vladimir Jabotinsky.

back either. Those who call *barzel* un-Jewish, those people whose Jewish educations were halted at age thirteen, know nothing of Judaism. Defending the Jewish people with physical strength is to understand "that when one deals with Esau, he must use the weapons of Esau" (p. 12). Nothing is forbidden when it is a question of saving a Jewish life. "The strength to be different," the strength to follow Abraham in refusing to conform, is also the strength of *barzel*. He who knows this can "stand up to the slings and arrows of his opponents and the protests of even those he loves" (p. 13). The frightened, assimilated diaspora Jew has not yet learned: "There is more to life than a job; there is more to existence than a meal" (p. 14). JDL members understand *barzel*, and in the translation of that understanding into action the JDLer is in the mainstream of Judaism.

(d) *Mishmaat Yisroel* ("Jewish discipline and unity")

The Jewish people can survive only when they are united and disciplined. Personal whims and political differences must be put aside "in the struggle for Jewish survival" (p. 14). Discipline is vital for JDL members, at meetings, at demonstrations, in following orders; this is our unity and strength. Above all, *mishmaat* is willpower from which stems the capacity to perform the impossible.

(e) *Bitachon* ("faith in the indestructibility of the Jewish people")

We have seen the great powers of the earth as our enemies; we have survived them all—"an Egypt, a Babylon, a Greece, a Rome, a Spain" (p. 15). Almost four thousand years ago the "All Mighty" promised Abraham that the Jewish people would become a "mighty nation." *Bitachon*, the faith that we shall overcome all enemies and emerge victorious, can only be faith in the Jewish people. No foreign power will help us. "At best, nations are motivated by self-interest, and we, the smallest of peoples offer little to the practitioners of realpolitik. At worst, there is a deep and abiding antipathy to the Jew, his cause, his land" (p.

15). Faith in the survival of the Jewish people also gives us faith that JDL will triumph. Our certainty becomes our success. Because we are right our "philosophy must emerge victorious" (p. 15).

Nationalism was incorporated in JDL Ideology by 1971, emphasizing *aliyah* as a religious obligation and as necessitated by the character of *galut*. The following paragraph from the "Movement Handbook" did not appear in the almost identical "Youth Movement Handbook" printed a year earlier:

> The Jewish people is a religious nation that came into being at Sinai. It is a special people with a special heritage and teaching, whose destiny it is to live in and to create within the land of Israel a society of holiness and greatness that will be an inspiration and example to the world (p. 3A).[4]

This is among the "positive reasons" for making *aliyah*: it is a sacred undertaking. "Negative Zionism" contains the second sort of "reason" for settling in Israel:

> . . . people, in the very best of times, do not like Jews and . . . people in America, today, do not like Jews . . . in the end we are left with Rabbi Shimon bar Yochai's resigned words: "It is a natural law that Esau hates Jacob. . . ." The place to hear and see this dislike is not at the hundred-dollar-a-plate banquet given by Jewish organizations to bestow a brotherhood award on a decent non-Jew. Those who dislike Jews, the nonfamous and the unknown, never come into contact with our patricians and leaders. They sit in their bars and in their modest

4 Orthodoxy defines Judaism as a religio-nation (the government of Israel is defined as a state rather than as the Jewish *nation*). Reform Judaism, particularly before World War II, minimized the notion of Jews as a "nation" and held Judaism to be a religion, like other religions. Several Zionist movements (e.g., many socialist Zionist groups) emphasized nationality, de-emphasizing religion.

homes and speak of: the Jews who are all communists; capitalism which is Jewish; the Jews who are bringing in the blacks; the Jews who own all the banks; the Jew as the internationalist Shylock . . ." (from "Jew Go Home," a JDL pamphlet).

And continuing:

As time goes on the chances increase that cultural anti-semitism will be picked up and used for political anti-semitism. That which happened in Germany can happen here . . . and the seeds of the holocaust are already sown. Will they grow into malignant choking vines that will strangle America? We do not know. We only know those who say that it can't happen here are fools or blind or both."[5]

The History around which the Ideology was built, beginning with Abraham, and including Theodore Herzl, Max Nordau, and Vladimir Jabotinsky among its "modern heroes," can be geometrically represented as an asymmetrical hourglass with the holocaust at the center. History after the holocaust reorganizes itself according to and toward the model of the ancient Jews. While the holocaust was seen as Historic, culminating in a new present, it was also potentially seen as repeatable. The memory and experience of the holocaust was posed as the key to the New Jew. Yet JDL Ideology asserted that the holocaust could be over-emphasized, thereby perpetuating the "image" of the Jew as unable to resist, as a "patsy," a "scapegoat." League

[5] Compare Hannah Arendt's *The Origins of Totalitarianism*. In particular: "[The 'anti-semitism is eternal' theory] stresses . . . with different arguments but equal stubbornness [as the scapegoat theory of anti-semitism], that complete and inhuman innocence which so strikingly characterizes the victims of modern terror, and therefore seems confirmed by the events. It even has the advantage over the scapegoat theory that somehow it answers the uncomfortable question: Why the Jew of all people?—if only with the question begging reply: Eternal hostility" (1958:8).

Ideology also highlighted the resistance that did occur under the Nazis—the Warsaw ghetto revolt, Hannah Senesh, who left Palestine to aid Jewish resistance in Eastern Europe, the uprisings at Treblinka and at Sobibor.[6]

"Ideology" included the league's formal Ideology as a symbol: JDLers believed their movement needed an Ideology; and Ideology, in turn, incorporated "ideology": Ideology expressly called for its own explication so that it would become believable and usable. Formal Ideology designated contexts in which Ideology was to be "taught" so that it might attain "relevance" to contemporary concerns. Timeless concepts like *ahavat Yisroel* and *hadar* demarcated the arenas for (JDL) action through the multiplication of concrete illustrations of their embodiment. In particular, examples of the absence of the "5 principles" among Jews were used to show the tragic consequences of ignoring "love of Jews," Jewish "pride," "strength," "unity," and "faith." Inaction of assimilated German and American Jewry in the years preceding and during World War II was recalled to illustrate the devastating result of not recognizing or of ignoring "Jewish problems." These examples were directly related by JDLers to present day assimilation and its potential consequences. JDLers viewed league Ideology as a conceptual counterpart to "action" (e.g., demonstrations), demanding action in general and justifying particular actions. Conversely, organized league "actions" substantiated Ideology and provided a forum where Ideology became "ideology" (individual JDLers' beliefs in themselves, JDL, Ideology, and the "historic" role of the league).

For JDLers the struggle to free Soviet Jewry represented the most outstanding fulfillment of league Ideology. Ideol-

---

[6] *They Fought Back,* edited by Yuri Suhl, and *Forged in Fury,* by Michael Elkins, about, respectively, resistance during the Nazi reign and Jewish revenge after the war were listed among those books JDL members were required to read.

ogy appeared to be speaking about facticity, and facticity to be responding to the enactment of Ideology's message. Universalistic premises of league Ideology seemed translatable into action, since the mission of Jewish "defense" was no longer being played out among a marginal group of Jews and their non-Jewish neighbors but had ascended the stage of world states and pan-national Jewry. The struggle was specifically Jewish and identified the people and the enemy in a global, contemporary, and tangible form.

The campaign against the Soviet Union enabled JDLers to combine within one context the "three or four things" they claimed they were "really fighting for." For instance, "physical defense," including the "harassment" of Soviet diplomats in the U. S. was used to "aid oppressed Jews" in their desire to make *aliyah*, thereby making available an attractive forum for the development of "Jewish identity." Freeing Soviet Jewry was the least impugnable—the "aim" if not the "tactic"—of JDL's several projects. Even the uncommitted American, Jew or non-Jew, could not easily criticize the right to free emigration. JDL consciously stressed various aspects of the struggle against the Soviet Union before different audiences: before religious Jews, the everlasting enmity of Communism and Judaism; before non-Jewish Americans, the dangers of Communist powers that "oppress Baptists and Jews together"; before Jews in general, the similarity of Soviet and Nazi treatment of Jews.

While acknowledging differences between physical and "cultural" extermination, JDLers referred to Nazi Germany and the Soviet Union as the "twin horrors of the twentieth century." Kahane writes:

> The list of Jewish enemies seems endless: Pharaoh, Assyria, Babylonia, Haman of Persia, Antiochus of the Greeks, Hadrian of the Romans, Christian fanatics throughout Europe and Asia Minor, Muslim fanatics in North Africa and in the Middle East, and finally, the twin horror of our own time, Nazi Germany and the

Soviet Union. These stand as a continual threat to the survival of the Jewish people, a threat which has been met by us in stubbornness, strength of purpose, and a tenacity which comes from Hadar and creates within us Hadar (1971:165-166).

Although the potential for physical extermination of Russian Jews was noted and the Stalinist period recalled, "cultural and spiritual" annihilation was seen as equally inimical to the "future of the Jewish people" as physical annihilation. Oppositions between "body" and "spirit" were not seen by JDLers as endangered in these assertions but rather doubly fulfilled: in this case, the spirit had to transcend the body; the tragedy of the loss of physical life was posited as the tragedy of spiritual death. Comparisons between Nazi Germany and the Soviet Union could be made *only because* of the body/spirit dichotomy. The Soviet Union had not yet done what Nazi Germany did, but its oppression was characterized as similarly severe—against spirit. Concomitantly, the existence of the chaya was justified as a bulwark against the destruction of the scholar. JDL's struggle for Soviet Jewry became the real proof of what could have been done in the 1930s to save the Jews of Europe. The History was seen to repeat and fulfill itself as "history" *for the sake of the scholar.* Kahane's book, *Never Again!*, has been faulted for glorifying Jewish life in pre-Communist Russia.[7] That glorification, however, reinforced

---

[7] For example, a review of *Never Again!*, printed in the *Jerusalem Post* (October 17, 1972) asserts: "Kahane's description of Jewish life in Russia of the Czars is over-romanticized: one is almost ready to burn the banner of Revolution and return the 'gentle' Romanoffs to power again. Surely Kahane knows the facts well, but in his attempt to make his point he distorts without batting an eyelash. . . . He fails to mention the Jewish bodies that littered the *shtetls* in Russia; those little boys snatched from their homes and conscripted into the Russian army during the reign of Nicholas I and then converted to Christianity; the Kishniev pogroms and the numerous other 'little pogroms'. . ." (Sharon 1972).

justifications for chayas' actions against the Soviet Union. The symbolic relation between chaya and scholar demanded that chaya did not encompass scholar. Additional chaya-ness could be condoned in defense of a truly authentic Judaism (or in defense against a powerful and evil enemy). If Russian Jewry before Communism epitomized traditional Jewish scholarship and that scholarship was posited as present, even if repressed, in contemporary Russian Jews, then chayas could hardly encompass this archetypical embodiment of the scholar.

JDL's formal Ideological axioms about a universal Jewish internality began to attain plausibility in the presence of a "true enemy" against whom "all kinds of Jews" were contending. Suddenly the particular cares of the poor, religious Jew, defended under the rubric of (Jewish) universalism really seemed to become part of an international project—one aspect of the general struggle to aid world Jewry. It was during this time that the two primary modifications in the nature of the league's active membership occurred: membership focus shifted from adults to youth,[8] and Jews who did not live in the neighborhoods where JDL's original activities began started joining the movement. There was an influx of wealthier and non-religious Jews, many of whom were teenagers and young adults. At least a score of active JDLers, who joined JDL during this period, claimed to have previously been members of leftist movements (e.g., SDS).[9] The league's Judaic authenticity and Jewish univer-

---

[8] Later JDL's leadership tried to re-orient the activities of the movement toward the interests, concerns, and capabilities of adult members.

[9] Almost all those JDLers who "came from the left" were naive about leftist thought, although several said they had spent as much time with the "left" as they were now spending with JDL. (JDL leaders said the design of the league office was consciously set up to emulate the offices of "typical" radical activist movements.) The reasons such persons gave for joining JDL did not differ much from those given by the more general members: a friend in JDL; observation of "anti-Semitism"—"ex-leftists" referred particularly to anti-Semitism among

salism were validated in the "obvious" prototypicality of the "enemy" (analogous to Historic anti-Semitism) and in the diversity of JDLers "demonstrating" together for the general "aim."

JDL has been held responsible, and JDLers have been indicted, for bombing Soviet properties in the U. S. and for other felonies in connection with the campaign against the Soviet Union, but the daily effort to augment or sustain attention to the Soviet Jewry issue was concentrated around public demonstrations; the majority of these demonstrations took place in New York near the United Nations or the Soviet Mission to the U. N. or in Washington. As a form of collective participation, demonstrations provided a framework for negotiation between levels of ideology and of history. Ironically the conceptions that extended meaning to demonstrations, coming from History and Ideology, were (re-)transformed in "action" into history and ideology. Or, to emphasize another aspect of the same process, within the context of demonstrations (within the planning, the enactment, and the subsequent assessment), the processes of "historicization" and "ideologization" occurred. JDL's stated, explicit intent was to enact Ideology, following the models of History. Inevitably the Historic and Ideological forms were subsumed as content within American forms of public demonstration, though this process was generally not noted by JDLers. JDL's intent was to embody universal Jewish internality (Jews acting like "Jews" for all Jews), but JDL demonstrations were like other demonstrations; the result was particularisitic externality (*some* Jews acting like other Americans). The remainder of this section considers JDL's attempt to mediate the internal and the external. Demonstrations, an exemplary arena for the contrast *and* combi-

---

leftist and/or black militant groups; seeing a JDL demonstration, ad, or success ("they seemed to be the only group doing anything for Soviet Jewry"); a parent who tolerated "radical action" if it was for a "Jewish cause."

nation of internality and externality, provide a frame of reference within which the following discussion can be contextualized.

JDL demonstrations did not look different from the demonstrations of anti-war protestors, black activists, the radical left, and so on; even the content of many slogans was interchangeable (e.g., "Freethem Now. Freethem Now. . . ."—American Blacks? Soviet Jews? Prisoners-of-War? Criminals? Heroes? You and me?). If one was not privy to the innuendos of language used in demonstrations, it was often possible to witness a demonstration and come away unsure who was demonstrating for what. The substitutability of the demonstration tactic was strikingly evident at a demonstration in front of the Israeli Mission to the U. N. (late 1971) involving JDL, a couple of "radical" Zionist groups (e.g., Radical Zionist Alliance), and a contingent of people demonstrating against Israel's position in the Middle East. At first the various groups mingled on the east side of Second Avenue, where the mission stands. After about an hour, city police cordoned off several areas. One policeman, herding demonstrators into "their area," said to three recalcitrant JDLers, "You can stand there and make as much noise as you want, but stand over there . . . where you belong. . . ." People demonstrating against Israel's position stood beneath the mission, facing JDL and the radical Zionists, themselves more or less segregated in a north-south direction on the west side of Second Avenue. Bullhorns carried the messages of antagonism east and west across the street. JDLers spent much of the demonstration trying to "develop a strategy" to break the "deadlock." After an hour and a half almost the entire group of JDLers crossed the street, continued east along 43rd Street, past the "anti-Israel" demonstrators, and proceeded to walk around the block. They were followed by about a dozen policemen, one of whom explained that the walk around the block was a JDL effort "to get the Arabs on the other side of the street." At this point one woman, demonstrating with the Radical Zionist Alliance declared, "Those anti-Israel people just don't understand. They don't understand. . . . But what I don't understand is how did we get to be on the same side of the street as JDL. They're just like the Black Panthers. . . ."

Demonstrations became another system of floating signs. For the purposes of public presentation JDL began to encourage individualistic modes of dress—from hasidic to "hip." Lefebvre writes of fashion (following the work of Barthes 1967) to illustrate the substitutability of signs (see chapter two above). Speaking of the modern "fascination of signs," he writes: ". . . floating in swarms and clouds they are free for all, ever available and, taking the place of action, they appropriate the interest formerly invested in activity" (1971:119). This may seem a curious quotation, since I am considering action, but demonstrations became a curious form of action, one that is easily generalizable. And fashion is not just an analogous system of sign substitutions; it became an important part of JDL demonstrations. The obvious question arises: what *is* being said with demonstrations and more specifically with the demonstration of array? If difference in dress is taken to signify difference in belief, then what is the basis of Ideological commonality? But if difference in dress is taken to signify difference in nothing (else), then why all the fuss?

Displays of sartorial variety mediated JDL internality and externality and indicated two JDL stances in public presentations, one before non-JDL Jews and the other before non-Jews. Before other Jews varieties of dress suggested that it was possible for a Jew "no matter what he does, no matter what party he votes for" to be represented by JDL; the JDL position looked like an internal (universal) position for any Jew. In the words of one non-JDLer, whose synagogue was "protected" by JDL after threats of "violence" had been voiced against the building (1970):

> . . . JDL came down the street marching and they came
> down singing. . . . I was very proud to be a Jew at this
> particular moment. Then more singing . . . some of them
> wore yarmulkas. Some of them wore dungarees. Some of
> them, real Yeshiva garb. Some of them looked like hip-
> pies. Some of them like hasidim. It was a real mixture of
> Jews, all kinds. Suddenly my emotions were so much
> involved; we are not as alone and as neglected. . . . All
> kinds of Jews were helping us. . . .

Before non-Jews the same move became a holding action
against American assimilation. JDL clothes and JDL demonstrations were not singularly or even particularly Jewish;
much of the league's early press coverage emphasized that
Jews could also "demonstrate," but the attention was on the
appropriation of an American form and not the presentation of a "Jewish" form. If, however, Jews were projected as
internally completing the normative order, then JDL could
stress that the Jewish community was analogous to, rather
than part of, the American socio-cultural order. Valorization of the collective whole (JDL), which (via "fashion")
represented all Jews, fulfilled the symbolic paradigm of
self-identity (based in substance) defended in the image of
the Other. The effort to sustain separation was publicly
carried out through forms that fostered assimilation; JDLers
saw this, but by showing that all Jews could demonstrate
with JDL, they posed the universality of the (Jewish) Self
as a deflection against assimilation with the Other. Modes
of showing both divergence from the identity of the Other
and from self identity were materially synonymous. If you
can "say it with clothes," the only privilege left is to think
you know what you are saying.

At demonstrations JDLers believed that Ideology was
being applied to reality in confronting the non-Jew (or
the non-JDL Jew) with demands for emending a particular
Jewish plight. Most of what occurred at demonstrations was
specific to demonstrations and not to JDL or Jews. In con-

junction with marching—generally moving as a group in circles—and civil disobedience, such as blocking traffic by sitting in city intersections, the focus of non-violent (parts of) demonstrations was songs and sayings communicating the group's message. Like other movements JDL had a repertoire of jingles, rhymed aphorisms, and paeans, forming the ordered verbalizations of demonstrations. Although even many of these explicit statements were interchangeable between groups demonstrating for discrepant causes, chants and songs offered a medium for expressing internality more than other aspects of a demonstration. Despite Jewish or "JDL" content, a chant was still in part a chant, emblematizing the unity of the group (e.g., *"Am Yisroel Chai; Od Avenu Chai,"* a well-known song meaning "The people of Israel still live. Our father still lives") and/or a communal statement symbolizing demands (e.g., "1-2-3-4 open up the iron door; 5-6-7-8 let our people emigrate"). JDL's song, "Never Again," was sung at least once and often several times at almost every league demonstration.[10] A millennial ring accompanied many of the slogans and songs, saying in

---

[10] The words to the song, "Never Again," written by a JDLer are:

CHORUS: Never again, Never again is our cry.
             Never again, Never again we vow,
             For we will do what must be done,
             And we will do it now.

VERSES: We proud sons of the Maccabees
            Stand up for Jewish right.
            Bar Kochba's blood fills our veins.
            We fear no mortal might.

            In Warsaw's ghetto we arose
            For our heroic stand,
            And then we threw the British out
            Of our holy land.

            You tyrants listen everywhere,
            Don't trample Jewish right,
            For when our brothers are oppressed,
            The JDL will fight.

translation, "History is now, and we move toward Utopia" (an "historic moment").

One chant used by JDL and built on a song known to and used by many Jewish youth groups (and heard at Jewish summer camps) deserves to be considered in some detail, since its structure allows greater flexibility than most chants. It involves a leader whose shouts are answered by the demonstrators as a whole. Although theoretically any demonstrator could start it, almost invariably the person who initiated this chant at league demonstrations was also a leader within the movement. The first few calls and responses are standard. The leader calls out in Hebrew, *"Abba"* (father); the group responds *"Ima"* (mother). The next five leader-group interactions are as follows:

Leader:	Ima
Group:	Abba
Leader:	Abba-Ima
Group:	Ima-Abba
Leader:	Ima-Abba
Group:	Abba-Ima
Leader:	Abba-Ima-Ima-Abba
Group:	Ima-Abba-Abba-Ima
Leader:	Ima-Abba-Abba-Ima
Group:	Abba-Ima-Ima-Abba

After this, JDL's chanting generally departed from the standard song; the league adopted forms of leader-group responses in which the followers answered *Yisroel* (Israel) to the leader's naming a series of places, farther and farther away from Israel, literally and figuratively. Frequently the chant ended with the leader saying "Yisroel," the group responding, as they had been, "Yisroel," followed by leader and followers together singing *"David Melech Yisroel, Chai, Chai v'kayam"* ("David, King of Israel, lives and endures"). A version chanted several times at a JDL demonstration for

Soviet Jewry in Washington, D. C. (1972) included the following calls (after the "Abba-Ima" calls):

Leader:	Yisroel
Group:	Yisroel
Leader:	Yerushalayim (Jerusalem)
Group:	Yisroel
Leader:	Tel Aviv
Group:	Yisroel
Leader:	Leningrad
Group:	Yisroel
Leader:	Auschwitz
Group:	Yisroel

The last call of the leader ("Auschwitz"), an unusual conclusion, one I had never heard before, was repeated several
times during the course of the demonstration.[11] Despite the
connotations of Never Again and comparisons between the
Soviet Union and Nazi Germany, JDLers did not generally
refer explicitly to the holocaust in the spontaneous order of
demonstrations.[12] Although the demonstration in which
this version of the "Abba-Ima" chant occurred was not in
the final analysis deemed a success by JDLers, the stage at
which the chant occurred was a period of emotional build-
up. Most of the demonstrators had driven to Washington
from New York, Boston, or Philadelphia, and the entire
group of demonstrators, who had assembled at a Washing-

[11] A version more commonly heard at JDL demonstrations is as
follows: Leader: Yisroel; Group: Yisroel. Leader: Yerushalayim; Group:
Yisroel. Leader: Tel Aviv; Group: Yisroel. Leader: Shchem [on the
West Bank]; Group: Yisroel. Leader: Cairo; Group: Yisroel. Leaders:
Moscow; Group: Yisroel.

[12] Just this sort of reference to the holocaust "in the streets of
Washington" was especially discomforting to many non-(anti-)JDL
Jews. In the words of one New York rabbi, "The holocaust is an un-
believably difficult thing to deal with or understand. I am sickened by
Meir Kahane and his little boys running around screaming 'neveragain-
neveragain.'"

ton park, had just embarked on a march from the park to the White House. Rumors were spreading through the group that "something" would happen at the White House. (In fact, the demonstrators met a cordon of policemen to whom they sang "*Hatikvah*," the Israeli national anthem, and "Never Again," the JDL song, and then straggled back to the park.) Several JDLers, speaking later of the version of the "Abba-Ima" chant that had been voiced, disagreed about the propriety of including references to the holocaust. The argument ceased when one participant asserted, "You schmucks can sit here and talk . . . but if there was a JDL then, there'd be six million more Jews today." In retrospect the chant, though having come close to a limit of propriety, had expressed something important for JDLers, and it is worth looking at how.

The initial "Abba-Ima" calls express a part/whole relation within the family (Mother-Father-Father-Mother) and an essential identity of part with part and of part with whole. Doublings of the initial "Abba-Ima" to include two and then four mothers and fathers signify an identity of each family with every family, reaching a culmination in "Yisroel-Yisroel"; the nation and the family are essentially equivalent. The structure is continued and the content spiritualized in "Yerushalayim-Yisroel," Jerusalem being the capital of the State of Israel and the religious center of Judaism throughout time. "Tel-Aviv," although part of Israel, begins the process of moving away from the center, for Tel-Aviv cannot stand for the spiritual state. With "Leningrad" there is a shift in the nature of the content, but the structure still allows a part/whole relation in the double sense that the Jews of Leningrad are also "Abba-Ima" (the Jewish people) and the enemy (here, Russia) can be overcome by "Israel" (JDL) in the fight to save (Soviet) Jewry. ("Israel" encompasses through sheer endurance.) In the last interaction, "Auschwitz-Yisroel," the Jews who died in the holocaust are spiritually reintegrated with "Israel." In that call the Nazis, signified by Auschwitz, can no longer be literally overcome, but there is a symbolic incorporation of the past within the present (an "historic moment"); this can occur because the "Leningrad-Yisroel" and "Auschwitz" calls maintain the part/whole structure while admitting opposition in content. Through the entire chant there is a progressive movement from the logically part/whole (member of family/family) to the psychologically part/whole in combination with the psychologically opposite (cf., Ogden 1932). The continued (leader/group-part/whole) structure of the chant through this shift in meaning allows the logic of the earlier relations to invade the psychological opposition of the later relations. "Leningrad-Yisroel" is the mediating call since the future orientation of the relation between Russia and Israel (JDL) allows the possibility of real overcoming; the overcoming of Russia could in fact presage the unification of Soviet Jewry and Israel. After this accomplishment, within and as witnessed by this demonstration, the opposition between Auschwitz (Jewish tragedy and non-Jewish brutality) and Israel (revitalization of Jewish strength and hope) is symbolically transcended through the re-creation and reversal of the holocaust in the struggle against the Soviet Union. The History from which the opposition (Auschwitz/Israel) stems is transposed; in this new symbolism, the Jew emerges stronger than past sufferings, and JDL provides a mediation of past and future, toward the reintegration of the largest Jewish community.

Concretely, through the particular demonstration JDLers could create links between themselves and the a priori meaningful panorama of History. To JDLers it began to look possible to use the tactic of the "militant," the "ethnic," the non-Jew, while preserving and enhancing a separate and authentic Jewishness. Even the spirit of Judaism, the religion, was described as present in demonstrations, almost intentionally suggesting a new form of religious ritual.

Althusser has characterized ideology as being simultaneously illusion and allusion; while entailing illusory relations to reality, ideologies also do allude to reality (1971:

153). An analogy stated by Kahane, relating JDL demonstrations to authentic and religious Judaism is particularly telling. By analyzing this analogy, we can examine JDL's manipulation of the allusion so as to sustain Ideology's illusions, the process through which Ideology was brought home as true to JDLers, and the process through which JDL created an internal identity that contrasted with the external identities of other groups (cf., Barnett n.d.). The analogy, though convincing to the audience before whom it was offered, was based on a fundamental paradox within JDL's constructed identity. To closely paraphrase Kahane, who was speaking at a resort in the Catskills about a JDL-led demonstration in Washington, D. C. (March 1971) where about 1,000 persons were arrested:

> You should have seen the shining faces of the JDL members as they sat in the streets of Washington waiting to be arrested. Then you would have seen what it means to be proud of being Jewish. For those kids *that* was a Bar Mitzvah. . . . I want especially to talk to the youngsters here. We hope to see you real soon in some jail! . . .

In analogizing JDL's demonstration to a Bar Mitzvah, the league's activity is compared with one of the most significant events in the life-cycle of the American Jew, an event signifying passage from childhood to full religious responsibility and privilege. Yet the way Americans celebrate the Bar Mitzvah is scorned by JDLers. Kahane writes:

> The Judaism of Scott's [any assimilated American Jew] parents, the Jewish culture to which they wished him exposed, consisted primarily of two things: Making sure their son came home with a Shirley instead of a Mary and seeing to it that their offspring would be properly sacrificed to the Great American Jewish god, the caterer, in that unique temple rite known as the Bar Mitzvah (1971: 123).

This is a characteristic JDL move. The Bar Mitzvah is highly important to the American Jew, often serving as the only religious ritual in which the Jewish male participates between circumcision at birth and burial in a Jewish cemetery at death. Yet Bar Mitzvahs are not required by Jewish law. At thirteen the male, and at twelve the female, automatically gain the rights of Jewish adulthood. The form in which this event has come to be celebrated is custom, not law. JDL's evoking the Bar Mitzvah as analogous to political activism turned accepted custom on its head but in a way that, if it came to it, could be justified through Talmudic reference and Biblical verse. JDL reasserted its central position as a modern counterpart to "Moses" through the Bar Mitzvah, and the Bar Mitzvah reemerged through JDL in an entirely new form, but as authentic as ever. The present was parodied; the past, hallowed; and JDL represented the second in the language of the first.

Ramifications of the analogy go beyond the represented synthesis of past and new present. Unlike the religious Bar Mitzvah ceremony, a distinctly individualistic commemoration—though group Bar Mitzvahs do occur, and the double or triple Bar Mitzvah has become common at many American synagogues and temples, for lack of enough Sabbaths in the year—the Bar Mitzvah "in the streets of Washington" was a massive affair, saluting the individual rite of passage *and* the coming-of-age of the American Jew—the chaya in *galut*. The synthesis of past and present is paralleled by the substantialization of the past (of History) so that past is presented as, in fact, made of the same stuff as, the present. A somewhat more careful look at the Bar Mitzvah analogy, apparently straightforward but actually loaded with meaning, serves as a lead into the way Ideology is appropriated by the individual JDLer (as "ideology"); this process, the effecting of the "real" from what is obviously a self-consciously created Ideology, is in and of itself paradoxical.

Examination of the Bar Mitzvah analogy reveals the concretization of that paradox.

The analogy contains terms indicating two kinds of activity, which I shall call the religious Bar Mitzvah and the political Bar Mitzvah: The first represents the maligned character of "authentic" religious Judaism; the second represents the "real" effecting of that Judaism, a stipulation dependent on the contiguity JDL presumes between its identity and that of Historic heroes—undeniably, intone JDLers, people of "authentic" Judaism. The analogy was limited by JDL's need to maintain identification with the Jewish people as a whole, including those people of whom the analogy was critical. Contemporary American Jewry, for instance, could be parodied but not cut off in that JDLers presumed their potential, rightful constituency to have included "all Jews."

Relations between the terms in the analogy can be formalized by employing Jacques Lacan's transposition of Ferdinand de Saussure's model for the representation of relations between signifier (S) and signified (s). In Lacan's formula (1968:105) the "signifier over the signified" (S/s) establishes the "signifying structure" from which meaning emerges and in which meaning is repressed. Initially, there are two primary terms, the religious Bar Mitzvah and the political Bar Mitzvah, with the second signifying the "authentification" of the first. However, for JDL the two sorts of Bar Mitzvah must remain in one domain, the domain of the "Jew"; to say this somewhat differently, the relation between the religious Bar Mitzvah and the political Bar Mitzvah is between two signifiers, or, following Seitel's definitions of metaphor and metonymy, takes a metonymic form.[13]

The metonymization of relations, in a formal sense, can be taken to imply creation of the "real," for metonymy

[13] Definitions of metaphor and metonymy employed here are from Seitel (1972). See chapter two above for those definitions.

entails contiguity and occurs in time. This is not so for metaphor, a relation that is fundamentally ahistoric. To get a little ahead of the case but in the hope of indicating where the present discussion is going, Kahane's analogy about the Bar Mitzvahs can be well characterized as an attempted metonymization of metaphor. And this attempt to transform Ideology into "ideology," to provide a grounding for Ideology, relies on the reification of the analogical.

Formally, the analogy states a metaphoric relation between the two signifiers, but the attempt of the analogy is to do this *without placing them in separate domains.* The religious Bar-Mitzvah, according to JDL, is supposed to represent the coming-of-age of the individual male Jew, but, as practiced in America, it does not. The analogy is created in the assertion that the league really does through the political Bar Mitzvah what is presumed by "assimilated" American Jewry to occur in religious Bar Mitzvahs. Religious Bar Mitzvahs are said to represent Jewish adulthood but are, according to JDLers, generally more akin to social extravaganzas than to religious commemorations. In other words, in terms of the analogy, the religious Bar Mitzvah is held to be a spurious signifier for the signified coming-of-age; it pretends—and fails—to adequately represent Jewish adulthood. Following the analogy, this signified (coming-of-age), falsely commemorated in religious Bar Mitzvahs, is *actualized* in JDL's political Bar Mitzvah, posed as synonymous with coming-of-age; at this point, the political Bar Mitzvah becomes a signified[14]—that is "real." A preliminary formulation of these relations can be diagramed as follows:

religious Bar Mitzvah (S) . . . political Bar Mitzvah (S^1)
———————————————————————————
coming-of-age (s)

Lacan calls the line in his diagram (S/s) between the signifier and the signified the "bar of signification" (1966,

---

[14] For Lacan all signifieds are at some level signifiers.

1968). Once the concept, political Bar Mitzvah, "crosses the bar" of signification to become a signified, the metaphor is again metonymized; that is, the political Bar Mitzvah of JDL and coming-of-age are now in the same domain. This is the necessary step before "what is not said" can be implied: that by *actually* being a coming-of-age of the American Jew, the JDL demonstration begins a return to the possibility of a real Bar Mitzvah, the traditional Bar Mitzvah of the scholar—the chaya is for the scholar in that the existence of the chaya can be legitimated by postulating the survival of the scholar to be dependent upon the actions of the chaya. The commemoration of that event occurs in the very formation on the analogy.

In short, a league demonstration, not visibly different from the demonstrations of almost any other American group, was posed as being closer to authentic religious ritual than what contemporary American Jews take as their religious ritual per se. For JDLers, the league was a reality and a symbol—the symbol often identified or confused with the "person," Kahane—and as a symbol JDL became a representation of self, thereby making every JDLer a part of the domain of "history" (history becoming History). In History the stressed opposition between Jew and anti-Semite is abstract. JDL had to transcend that opposition while endowing it with contemporary names and faces. The league's expressed aim was the overcoming of anti-Semitism, but that task, modeled on History, depends on the existence of anti-Semites. The creation of group identity entails the construction of the interior and of the exterior—of those persons and groups who are Other (Sartre 1963). And within the substantial "universe" of the West, where groups become metaphors for each other, the metonymizations endowing the interior with a sense of "history," a sense of being "real," become easily appropriable by other groups—thus the substitutable character of "ethnicity" (cf., Barnett n.d.).

One JDLer, who considered himself a scholar within the league, spoke of his self-identification as a JDLer. Here is manifest a definition of internality (with no sense of the eventual deflection):

> JDL is like a mirror for me. . . . I've done things in JDL which haven't won the admiration of all my next door neighbors and my parents' friends, because all I hear from them is "You're killing your parents," or things of that sort. Like my mother says, "I'm getting a heart attack," which I feel very bad about. But JDL has made me realize, has shown me a place, an important place . . . at least so far. . . . I'm not exactly the quiet type, but JDL—I can look at myself through it, through what it is . . . the whole of JDL . . . it has given me a place to identify with. . . . [It is] the part of Judaism that is the most difficult [to enact] . . . I can look at the chayas. They're terrific, the best part of JDL are the chayas, but I think I can do more important things than that in JDL . . . but that's what JDL is, together. . . .

"JDL," said the speaker, "is like a mirror. . . ." In the mirror is both JDL (scholar-chaya) and this JDLer. Through the image in the mirror—in Lacan's term,[15] through the other of the self—the whole is reconstituted within the individual. The speaker continued, "in JDL you can really see history. And even to be part of history." In this mirror relationship JDL is at its most personal and its most abstract; with self reflected through one side and History through the other, JDL's ideal symbolic construct (see, chapter three) is re-enforced. JDL as a whole is representative of and reflected in each of its members.

Actualization of scholar and chaya (as in a demonstration) validates History, providing models for "historicization." JDL's internality was effected through relations between self, group, and History; in History anti-Semitism does not have to be proved, for it is obvious. Indeed many

---

15 The postulation of a mirror is also suggestive in light of the significance Lacan attaches to the *stade du miroir* (mirror phase) for objectification of self in the development of the child (1966, Vol. 1).

Jews (and non-Jews) not in favor of JDL saw truth in the league's outline of history. "They are crazy," said one anti-JDL New York rabbi, "but history is on their side." Through the substantialization of History, individual JDLer, JDL, and History become synonymous, and thus Ideology achieves its guarantee as "ideology" (cf., Althusser 1971). The Ideology, an Ideology that was consciously fabricated, begins to attain veracity. Eventually to deny the fabrication of Self is to deny self. In the words of one JDLer, "Everyone who cares about JDL is part of us. . . . JDL is also part of history. . . . Like take history books in a hundred years. JDL could be there in those books and if JDL is . . . then in a way each one of us will be also. . . ." The experience from within which that simultaneity of identifications is engendered is a leap of faith but is not unstructured. Creation of a (substantially) unified self/JDL/History occurs through the metonymization of metaphor: the merely comparable becomes the identical and yet remains a basis of comparison.

It would seem to be this relation (the metonymization of metaphor) that is implied by Freudian condensation.[16] Although several writers (e.g., Althusser 1971:191; Wilden 1968) have fully equated condensation with metaphor (and the contrasting process, displacement, with metonymy), the process of condensation would seem in fact to succeed only in the overcoming of metaphor. Condensation can be characterized as a *working through metaphor towards a prevailing over metaphor*. In condensation the relationship between structured elements in different domains becomes so powerful ("ideologically" convincing) that the domains themselves begin to merge. To repeat: the merely comparable becomes the identical. Or, in other words, what looks like form subsumes what looks like content.

---

[16] Compare Althusser 1969, 1971; Lacan 1966, 1968. Freud (1965) referred to the "compression" of the dream-content as "condensation." Lacan has explained this process as occurring in the structure of language, isomorphic with the structure of the "unconscious."

Returning to the Bar Mitzvah analogy, the structure of that analogy is founded on condensation, but that condensation entails contradictions. In the above diagram outlining relations within the Bar Mitzvah analogy, the political Bar Mitzvah moves across the bar of signification to become the coming-of-age. That diagram is correct insofar as it goes, but does not expose the full implications of the analogy (in condensation they may, as Lacan suggests, never be fully exposed). Following Lacan (1966, 1968), the bar between the signifier and the signified generates both movement ("the emergence of meaning") and resistance. In the statement of the Bar Mitzvah analogy—calling a political action a Bar Mitzvah—that action does not signify a coming-of-age. It *is* the coming-of-age. Resistance between signifier and signified, the struggle of meaning, is overcome through condensation by which the political Bar Mitzvah becomes an overdetermined symbol; however, and this is the vital point, this meaning was generated (its resistance worn out) only through invoking the prior relation between coming-of-age and the religious Bar Mitzvah, a Bar Mitzvah already taken to signify coming-of-age. The diagram can now be reformed accordingly:

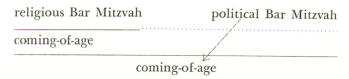

It is necessary to recall that the actual coming-of-age in the political Bar Mitzvah is only possible in opposition to the Other (the anti-Semite; in this case the Soviet Union). Yet the political Bar Mitzvah becomes the signified (the actualization of coming-of-age) only by accepting the terms of the religious Bar Mitzvah. In short, the need to define the political Bar Mitzvah (JDL) as authentically Jewish, thus removing the resistance to signification, assumes a model (the religious Bar Mitzvah) that signifies coming-of-age independently of the Other. The condensation is faced with the following contradiction: if the link (as signifiers in one domain) between the religious Bar Mitzvah and the political Bar Mitzvah is upheld, then there is no room in the process of identification for the Other, the anti-Semite. But since the identification of the political Jew is possible only through behavior vis-à-vis the anti-Semite, ignoring the Other is ignoring the Self. If, on the other hand, religious Bar Mitzvah and political Bar Mitzvah are placed in separate domains, then the authenticity of the political Jew (as religious Jew) is nullified.

A similar contradiction re-occurred, though in a somewhat different place, in JDL's "ideology" after nationalism became an official part of Ideology. As mentioned earlier, advocating *aliyah* entails a variant form of individualism than that entailed in sustaining an "ethnic" position in America. By 1971 JDLers hoped to maintain the league "defense" of diaspora Jews, while urging all Jews to emigrate to Israel. Symbolic forms of integration—internally and externally—that were beginning to emerge for JDL in America were undermined by growing stress on the individual-nation relation, and at the same time JDLers in Israel were attempting to sustain the ethnic models generated in the U. S.

The decision to become an actively "Zionist" movement was hotly debated within JDL. This issue, more than any other, caused rifts among JDL's leadership,[17] since a large proportion of JDLers, especially "adult" members, had seen the league as a defense against Jewish difficulties in America, as an example of the Jew "finally" demanding the right to stay. In supporting the necessity of massive emigration to Israel, JDLers began to emphasize the ultimate insolubility

[17] Intense debate had previously centered on the league's supporting the Vietnam War. That issue, in contrast with the debate about *aliyah*, was resolved with the decision to allow each JDLer, speaking publicly "as a JDLer," to voice an individual opinion.

of the extant "Jewish problems" in America,[18] and predicted a potential American counterpart to the Nazi holocaust. Few, if any, JDLers disagreed with this characterization of present difficulties or with the forebodings about the future. But to many JDLers that lack of disagreement, in and of itself, did not seem sufficient reason for "giving up the fight here in America." The Zionist "addition" to league Ideology was concomitantly explained as a further instance of JDL's "authentic" Jewishness, given traditional concern with the "natural" relation between the Jewish people and the land of Israel.

In general, "additions" to JDL Ideology could be taken as only an enlarging of Ideology and not in contradiction with extant Ideology if the additions were seen as coming from authentic Judaism (religion) and if religion was not itself seen to be in contradiction with "ideology." As noted in chapter three, the inclusion in JDL Ideology, rather than the origin in religion, could become the significant aspect of any Ideological dictum. Religion bestowed the initial authentification and later, when the belief was successfully inscribed in league Ideology, its origin in religion became less important. The league took great pains, however, to assure people (JDLers and non-JDLers) that, although JDL did not violate religious law, it was not a religious move-

[18] That the actual socio-economic position of the American Jew deteriorated sharply between 1968 and 1971 (between the origin of JDL and inclusion of nationalism in Ideology), as JDLers claimed, is not certain. Statistics are hard to come by, since the United States census does not ask religious affiliation. Herbert Bienstock, Regional Director, United States Department of Labor, suggested (1971) that although there were "fields of employment that seem to be closing down for Jewish young men and women" (e.g., "education, government, people-serving activities"), this reflects, at least in the case of education that "the 'self-decision process' was at work" (1971:36). Bienstock asserted that the relatively large proportion of Jews with college educations would become a less decided asset as more Americans in general received college degrees, and Bienstock proposed that Jews should try to gear more of their young for employment in blue-collar occupations.

ment. Religion was posited as the spiritual force that stood behind the Historic heroes, the heroes whom JDLers embodied in their present. Dexterous use of religious authority enabled the authentification of a self-identification that had little to do with religion per se. As long as JDL claimed not to be a religious movement, religion could emerge at the level of belief, though not of practice, as undisputed authority. When nationalism became part of league Ideology, the religious mandate was not enough to legitimate what was disputed on other grounds. Consequently religion itself became a source of contention. When, by 1972, JDLers were asked by non-JDL Jews whether it was not quite as dangerous to live in Israel as, say, in Brooklyn, Orthodox members began to respond by insisting on the need for "faith." To paraphrase Kahane:

> Logically, perhaps, that can't be disputed, but we have faith in God. The Talmud talks about two destructions [the destructions of the first and second Temples] but not of three. We have faith that Israel will survive.

At this point religion is no longer submerged in JDL Ideology; Ideology is being held together by religious faith. The difference between reliance on religious authority (as History) and being a religious group begins to blur with that kind of "faith."

The difference between acting like a Jew (Historic hero) through opposition to anti-Semitism and being a Jew through faith has parallels in the difference between stress on identification as an ethnic group and stress on identification as a cultural and territorial national group. Barnett and Barnett (1974), considering change toward individualism (class, ethnicity, and so on) in the Indian caste system, define nationalism as follows:

> . . . territorial nationalism in the pure form posits only the self (and other equivalent selves) and the nation.

There is no ranking here, only equivalent selves agreeing to unite in a bounded physical space. And so there is a tension between ethnicity and nationalism—between self and nation, and self, intermediary groups, and nation. Unlike ethnicity, cultural nationalism does not see a plurality of groups constituting a nation but one culture equating one nation, adding a code for conduct requirement to nationhood (1974:47).

The valorization of the collectivity in the context of American ethnicity was confounded by the stipulation of nationalism, for now JDL, the ethnic "intermediary," was really *not* necessary. Conversely the valorization of each individual in Israel vis-à-vis the nation was confounded by the attempt to sustain JDL as a "non-political" ethnic mediator, according to a model developed in the context of the American non-Jew.

By 1972 the league, in attempting to maintain itself as an American ethnic mediator and as quintessentially Jewish, was making official decisions that undermined that very attempt, e.g., the decision to admit non-JDLers and even non-Jews into the chaya squad. This decision, made after Kahane had been intermittently in Israel for about a year, is mentioned in chapter three as an illustration of (the failure of) the second precept of JDL's symbolic construct (chaya: scholar :: non-Jews: JDL). JDL justified this decision, saying it was vital to maintain a viable chaya squad, but in consequence the possibility of ethnic separation was symbolically negated. Admitting non-Jews into the squad, however, had ceased representing the "end of the Jewish people," since the essence of that people was being re-defined in terms of a self-nation relation. It did signify the encompassing of "identity" in "image" in America and the absorption of an American JDL into the dominant society. Intentions of the motto, "Never Again," were altered: no longer through defense in *galut*, but through emigration to Israel, could the Jew provide self-protection. "Never Again" came to mean Not Here in Israel, an affirmation supported in "faith."

When JDL first opened offices in Israel, the league declared itself a potential "bridge" among Israelis. Before the inclusion of nationalism into league Ideology, JDLers in America had characterized the abstract Israeli as the prototypical scholar-chaya; JDL was to be an American embodiment of the Israeli, providing that in *galut* the Jew (the scholar) could be a chaya. As Kahane was metaphorically JDL, so JDL was metaphorically Israel. When JDL established its international headquarters in Jerusalem, the league's aim was to provide a forum for the resolution of internal Israeli conflict by representing all Israelis as a non-political "bridge." The model around which this aim was to be enacted, however, was the ethnic model built around the relation between Jews and American non-Jews and stressing a contrast between assimilation and separation. It was hardly appropriate for a nationalist group *in* its nation. Several individual JDLers recognized contradictions between their relation to JDL, the ethnic mediator, and their relation to the Israeli nation. By late 1971 a number of active JDLers were beginning to voice, along with the decision to make *aliyah*, the determination to curtail their involvement with JDL when they settled in Israel. In the words of one JDLer:

> Once I get there I won't have anything to do with JDL. Are you kidding me? I've had it. . . . I may not even see them when I get there. . . . JDL may have a goal in Israel . . . I'm not sure, but that's it for me with JDL. Not in Israel. I want to be an Israeli, not a JDLer. . . .

The nationalist relation is between "the self (and other equivalent selves) and the nation" (Barnett and Barnett 1974); there was no room for JDL, the ethnic intermediary. In late 1972 the league reversed its earlier vows never to become a "political party" in Israel and declared its intention to run candidates for the Israeli Knesset, the decision having been attributed to "harassment" from the Israeli government.

During the winter of 1971-1972 the league began to make plans for establishing a JDL kibbutz and kiryat (JDL town). Although neither of these proposals has been enacted, they were geared toward the development of a unified and "non-political" JDL within the Israeli context, and incorporated the belief in JDL as prototypically "Israeli." JDL hoped to build the kibbutz in the "liberated territories" (the land annexed to Israel after the Six-day War). Both the kibbutz and the kiryat were planned to include among their residents recent emigrés from America and from the Soviet Union as well as longer term Israeli citizens including *sabras* (native born Israelis). More significantly, the living arrangements were to provide for the needs of religious and non-religious people. The *dati* (religious)/*lo dati* (non-religious) split in modern Israel is a source of constant difficulty and conflict, and extant Israeli settlements are either religious or non-religious; few non-religious people live on religious settlements, and fewer religious people live on non-religious settlements. JDL saw a league kibbutz and kiryat as potential avenues for enabling the consolidation of the everyday and the heroic, as places to "*live JDL.*"

Although the league kibbutz and kiryat have not materialized, the JDL camp in the Catskills (summers 1969-1971) and school in Israel (summer 1972) offer two instances of JDL communal living; both, however, involved only "youth." At the camp, and even more so at the school in Israel, the group was physically removed from American non-Jews (and "anti-Semites"), whose existence necessitated Jewish "defense." Identity could not, in short, be constantly re-asserted through daily interaction with the Other. Both situations involved a fair amount of religious disputation that is relevant to the differences between ethnic and nationalist individualism. The majority of participants at the camp and the school came from religious backgrounds. A minority of about one-fourth was quite religious, and a somewhat smaller minority was non-religious; a few among this latter group were out-spokenly against the observance of religious law and custom. Theoretically, living arrangements were supposed to reflect a "compromise" between two extreme positions. Religious law (e.g., kashrut, shabbot) was to be observed at the school, for instance, within the buildings where the students lived, and permission was granted to non-religious students to "do whatever they want outside the school." All males were required to attend shachrit (morning prayer) and all students to attend shabbot services "unless someone finds it personally offensive to doven [pray]." (Despite incessant grumbles about "having to be religious," no one was ever willing to be declared as someone personally offended by religious observance.) To paraphrase a JDL leader, these requirements were warranted insofar as it was bad to risk splitting the group into two; it was necessary to have a *minyan* (ten males needed for public services), and participation in prayer was, at the very least, like attendance at another class.

While several non-religious students saw this "compromise" as an imposition on their "right not to be religious," some Orthodox students said, on the contrary, they were compromising their religious beliefs in knowing about and even witnessing several infractions of religious law within the school (e.g., using electricity or smoking on shabbot). One Orthodox student, in the midst of an argument with an "atheist" (the "atheist" student's own word) declared, "Well, it won't kill you to go to shule [synagogue]." The "atheist" countered, "Yeah, so. It won't kill religious people to eat shrimp." (Eating shellfish is proscribed by the laws of kashrut.) There is surely more involved in such altercations than the terms in which "compromise" could be effected. Conflicts over religious practice were not only pertinent to JDL's use of religious "authority" in justifying "political" practice (e.g., the use of violence), but were about political practice and belief, though the intersection of "religion" and "politics" in such contexts was disguised. It is important to note that conflicts about religion concerned the significance of ritual prescriptions or prohibitions but rarely the existence of God and never the validity of divine History. In the argument referred to above, both parties, whom I shall call Ellen and Milton, respectively the religious and the non-religious conversant (as well as several peripheral people who joined in on one side or the other during the dispute), explicitly disagreed about religious observance. It was assumed, however, that this disagreement was based in a "common scheme of interpretation" (Cicourel 1970:41). "I'd love to see all JDLers Orthodox," said Ellen, "but I know JDL is for all Jews, not just the Orthodox." Milton agreed and disagreed: "Right. . . . But we're not talking about JDL. I understand your point . . . but if your side ever won, I'd leave JDL." Despite the disclaimers, JDL was being talked about.

The "Judaisms" through which Ellen and Milton were relating to each other and to JDL as Jews were based on fundamentally variant conceptions. For the Orthodox Jew, links of contiguity are established with Biblical figures (of common ancestry) through a shared legal-ritual system, founded in divine sanction. The relation between self and nation (and other equivalent selves) defining (JDL's) nationalism was an easy step from the relation between self and religion ("land, people, heritage") pertaining in Orthodox Judaism.[19] The dichotomy posited in Orthodoxy between galut and Israel makes the shift from an ethnic to a nationalist relation relatively easy, since the structure of the nationalist relation is part and parcel of the religion. For the non-religious JDLer, on the other hand, the relation to "Judaism" (through JDL), based within the ethnic model, was more fully dependent on the existence of the non-Jew.

[19] Again, Schneider's suggestion that in America nationality and religion are structured similarly to kinship is suggestive (1969).

The models of code for conduct exemplified by Historic heroes are precisely behavior vis-à-vis non-Jewish enemies— Moses against the Egyptians, Judah Maccabee against the Greeks, Bar Kochba against the Romans, Hannah Senesh against the Germans, the Irgun and Lechi against the British. For the non-religious JDLer, interaction with the non-Jew ("anti-Semite") supported personal contiguity with shared History through JDL, the latest instance in a "chain" of Jewish resistance fighters. JDL's intention to establish the league's kibbutz within the "liberated territories" is of utmost significance. In planning the kibbutz, the league hoped to receive permission from the Israeli government to situate the settlement in either the Golan Heights or the West Bank; both areas were joined to Israel in 1967 and are populated largely by Arabs. Had such a kibbutz been set up it would have enabled the imagined sustenance of heroism dependent on "defense" against non-Jews, by providing a context for the apparent conjunction of ethnicity and nationalism—in the nation. As imagined, this was the amalgamation, par excellence, of the heroic and the quotidian. By presenting an image that appeared actualizable, and an image supplying the needs of any Jew because of the universality of its design, the notion of such a kibbutz once again substituted faith in self (JDL) for faith in God, as preeminent in the quest for a New Jerusalem.

League members' recognition that JDL "ideology" was a personal ideology—what Althusser calls ideology's guarantee—depended upon self-identification based in oppositions to the Other (the anti-Semite). Ties to the Historic heroes were both natural ties—extensions of the blood relation to the mother through which a person *is* a Jew—and ties of conduct. Behavior shared with Historic heroes, behavior opposing anti-Semitism, extended the natural familial relation so that Historic heroes could be included within the family. Similarly land (Israel) was posited as a substantial, shared tie among all Jews. Within the land of Israel, the natural home of the Jew, JDL presumed to enact essential Jewishness by representing all Jews and serving as a bridge among them. As soon as JDL opened offices in Israel, however, it was obvious that the league was not receiving general acclaim as *the* essential Jew. Identification had to come from elsewhere. Once again, the non-Jew was necessary as the Other against whom the Self could be defined; plans were set up to build JDL settlements in the Golan Heights or on the West Bank.

"Ideology's" guarantee is short-lived if not constantly re-affirmed and reflected in the here and now. Indeed the fact that the majority of people who became committed to JDL dissociated themselves from the league, in all but name at any rate, within six months to a year after joining bears witness to the difficulty of maintaining the guarantee. The anti-Semite of History must be situated in the daily present in order for Ideology to maintain its significance as "ideology." JDL's struggle for Soviet Jewry was at least momentarily efficacious in re-enforcing "ideology's" guarantee; the Soviet Union could be categorized as anti-Semitic with little dispute from American Jews, but perhaps more consequentially this anti-Semitism, unlike that attributed to non-Jewish Americans, was physically distant. JDLers did not themselves come into direct contact with the reality of Soviet anti-Semitism, so that the application of Ideology and its believability as "ideology" focused around an enemy who could be visualized apart from an everyday reality; there was, that is, great flexibility for JDLers in constructing an image of Soviet anti-Semites; in short, they could be imagined and described by JDLers as exactly like Historic anti-Semites.

The league was created, however, in "defense" against "anti-Semitism" in modern America. The preeminence of that defense was eclipsed for JDLers by the Soviet Jewry struggle but was never given up totally. In fact in 1972 league activities against the Soviet Union occurred less frequently and received less press coverage when they did occur than in the few preceding years. But league members believed they had demonstrated that characterizations of JDL as a marginal and disavowed part of the Jewish whole were misguided; concomitantly, when by 1972 JDLers discussed the Jewish situation in the U. S., they stressed the dim future facing all American Jews quite as much as the particular misfortune of certain Jews. The next chapter considers JDL's construction of Self vis-à-vis the Other within America and vice versa. The certainty and specificity with which the Soviet Union could be viewed as archetypically anti-Semitic was not possible regarding Others within the U. S. But in either case the definition and identification of anti-Semitism stood behind the permanence of "ideology's" guarantee; against the eternal *and* transcendable Other, the self united with other Selves (JDL) in making history "historic" and in believing that "history" was akin to History.

CHAPTER V

Silent Screaming

JDL Ideology "found itself" in a permanent opposition between the anti-Semite and the Jew, and most JDLers unhesitatingly upheld the dictum that all non-Jews were potential anti-Semites and all Jews, potential victims. This simplicity, however, concealed a significant variation in JDLers' beliefs about and interactions with different groups of non-Jews. Not unaware of these contrasting constructions of Self and Other, JDLers were caught in a pull between apprehending an unequivocal division of Jews and non-Jews and understanding a more complex universe of social interaction. The inclusion of nationalism into league Ideology, especially since that nationalism could be and was enacted through emigration, altered the sorts of relations relevant to JDLers' consciousness of the inter-ethnic situation. Advocating Zionism as not only a "luxury" but a "necessity" suggested that the opposition between Jew and non-Jew could not ultimately be mediated; however, JDL's earlier representations of relations between Jews and of various groups of non-Jewish Americans, as people with whom one had to live rather than from whom one has to depart, pertain to American ethnicity in a more general way. Before considering the modes of interrelation that JDL established and wanted to establish with relevant Others, I shall demarcate and in part reiterate the general framework of analysis.

Useful approaches to an examination of Western individualism stem from research on the structural universe of caste. Following Dumont (1970, 1965a) and Barnett (1973a, 1973b), one of the most suggestive aspects of caste hierarchy in comparison with Western stratification for an analysis of ideology is the relative transparency of the traditional caste system. To quote Dumont:

> The crux of the matter is that "exploitation" embodies, as few other terms do, an exclusively modern, individualistic and equalitarian viewpoint, and that its blunt application to a holistic and hierarchical society carries just as much meaning as the statement that the caste system denies the rights of man. . . . in this system [caste hierarchy] all receive *something*, and all receive according to their status; they receive unequally because they are conceived as unequal beings having unequal needs (1965a:88).

In the West transparency has been replaced by opacity, since inequalities attend an egalitarian ideology; the representation of relations between people and groups masks the facticity. The terms transparency and opacity are used by Marx; their meaning is well indicated in Marx's description of transparent relations obtaining between Robinson Crusoe and his world or between medieval Europeans and theirs:

> In spite of the variety of his work [Robinson Crusoe] knows that his labour, whatever its form is but the activity of one and the same Robinson, and consequently, that it consists of nothing but different modes of human labour. . . . All the relations between Robinson and the objects that form this wealth of his own creation, are here so simple and clear as to be intelligible without exertion. . . .
>
> Let us now transport ourselves from Robinson's island bathed in light to the European middle ages shrouded in darkness. Here, instead of the independent man, we find everyone dependent. . . . But for the very reason that personal dependence forms the groundwork of society, there is no necessity for labour and its products to assume a fantastic form different from their reality (1967:76-77).

In both cases the process underlying the creation of relations between the social order and the cultural order effects relations of transparency: the symbol systems of Crusoe and of medieval Europe allow an understanding of one's place in the scheme of social relations; similarly the hierarchical caste system is transparent in comparison to Western individualism: caste *is* inequality. The processes producing the processes of representation in the West effect opacity; indeed the notion of opacity well characterizes the individualist metaphoric universe in which, as Lefebvre puts it, anything can be anything (cf., Kemnitzer, n.d., for an extended discussion of the anthropological implications of transparency and opacity).

Barnett's documentation of the "ethnicization" of one South Indian non-Brahman upper caste points to the decreasing encompassment of the "conscious" features (cf., Dumont 1970)[1] of caste hierarchy toward the emergence of previously encompassed aspects of individualistic stratification, politics, and economy. This shift entails the move from relative transparency to relative opacity. The symbols (e.g., blood) defining caste hierarchy have been retained as elements in a profoundly altered structure. With caste hierarchy, blood and code for conduct are connected in the sense that transactions between castes (code for conduct) *are* natural identity. Substantialization of blood with the dissolution of the tie between natural identity and code for conduct means that the placement of a particular caste

[1] Dumont has suggested a model for comparison in which the conscious features of each system (e.g., hierarchy in India; equality in the West) are attended by less conscious features; he calls the first (the "conscious") features "substantive" (*S*) and the second, "adjective" (*a*), and suggests that the total features in one system are found in the other, with variant placement (i.e., more or less "conscious") making for drastic differences in the respective "universes." Explaining this "postulate for comparison" he writes, "This amounts in practice to saying that in any society there will always be found that which corresponds [in] a residual way (in *a*) to what another society differentiates, articulates and valorizes (in *S*)" (1970:340). This footnote has been included to indicate Dumont's consistent interest in comparison; the positivism of the specific model, however, is accepted only in a figurative sense.

within the hierarchical system is no longer part and parcel of code for conduct. Given such a shift, it becomes possible to retain "caste" (now ethnic) rank irrespective of transactional behavior, since identity inheres in the substance (blood) of the group, apart from other groups. Consequently, relative rank becomes disputable. An individual's actions do not necessarily implicate the larger "group" as a whole and, furthermore, behavior becomes emulatable among groups. The clarity of a group's place in the social whole is lost. The stressed features of substantialized caste and of Western stratification are directly comparable. The outstanding factor in the egalitarian ideology of the West is the valorization of the independent individual who is the focus of "rational" order, but as Dumont notes, the conception of individual independence ("freedom") at once entails absolute interdependence: "this ideally autonomous man was in actual fact the most dependent of his kind, tightly enclosed in an unprecedented extension of the division of labor" (1970:237). Holism, not absent from the individualistic universe, takes a form quite unlike that of caste hierarchy—the valorization of the "collective individual," that is, totalitarianism. Ethnicity, less inclusive than totalitarianism, is another variant of "individualistic" holism. The person, the group, and the nation can serve, in short, as metaphors for each other.

In the modern West, universalities imputed to the rational individual have served in an obdurate denial of the reality of inequality. "Without distinction of sex or birth," writes Marcuse, "regardless of their position in the process of production, individuals must subordinate themselves to cultural values. They must absorb them into their lives and let their existence be permeated and transfigured by them" (1968:94). American ideology has consistently stressed the possibility for the abstract individual to achieve the ideal success of socio-economic "escape" from "distinctions of sex or birth." Yet the very categories in terms of which that escape is measured have intransigently remained the categories of sex and birth—race, national origin, religion, and sex. There has been a curious tension within American ideology in the face of obvious inequalities. In what is one of the more remarkable exploits of "ideological history," American common sense has come to admit the injustices of socio-economic reality while insisting with consistent fervor that there is no imposition of (culturally defined) natural inferiority (racism). Western social science has presented numerous scaled attributes by which groups differentiated according to nationality, religion, race, and sex can be ranked within the social whole (e.g., economic mobility, political participation, education level, residence location). The preeminent consequence is the salience of rank disputation, with one exception: blacks tend to be ranked at the bottom of any scale, and this exception points to the difference between race and ethnicity: the relative rank of a race is less disputable than that of an ethnic group.[2] Recent attempts to equate black "progress" with ethnic "progress" may stem as much from the insistence of the egalitarian ideology in proving its own veracity as from fact.[3]

[2] See Barnett and Barnett (1974) for indications of the difference between emerging racial and ethnic groups in India: "race involves putative physical differences to an extent not shared by ethnicity," and additionally "racism implies a clear ranking not manifest in ethnic group separation" (1974:47).

[3] It is useful to take an illustration. Disagreements as to how black "progress" can be measured may themselves be suggestive. In an inflationary economy absolute income increase tells little. Given that, computations of the percentage gap between black and white income have been used as indices of black progress. As with any statistical representation, there are many ways to say the same thing, and inevitably relevant factors are omitted from the computations. An apparent close in the percentage gap between medium black and white income during the 1960s has been pointed to as an indication of black progress. According to the Bureau of Census reports, the largest decrease in the gap occurred between 1965 and 1966: medium black income was 50% of medium white income in 1965 and 58% in 1966 (*New York Times*, July 23, 1973). The *New York Times'* presentation of Census Bureau data indicates that the gap decreased slowly between 1966 and 1970, with medium black income being 61% of medium white income in

In the last several years, another and somewhat less disguised version of the tension in American ideology is evinced: black "ethnicity" is glorified and appropriated but simultaneously feared and turned aside. A great deal has been said about lower-middle-class white ethnic "backlash," but there has been little analysis at the cultural level as to what this "backlash" means. The notion "backlash" is used variously as a euphemism for and a denial of racism; although not generally stated in exactly this way, part of the "fear" imputed to white ethnics is that, should blacks become another "ethnic" group, then relative rank would be absolutely disputable; the insecurity of the white ethnics or "middle-Americans" regarding their (group's) place in the scheme of socio-economic things would be total. In this light JDL presents a key case, since the league began in large part as a "defense" against emerging "black power" but quite soon took up the very tactics that had been vehemently condemned in the movement's own earliest pamphlets and public statements. The first leaflets put out by JDL posed "radical action"—"civil disobedience"—as an indicator of "political extremism." Within a year radical action was offered as evidence of Jewish authenticity, and JDL was proudly underscoring its difference from the Jewish "estab-

---

1970. In the last two years the gap has increased one percentage point each year: it was 59% in 1972. Being neither a statistician nor an economist, I do not want to dispute the facts of the case, as it were, but only to suggest that reports in the *New York Times*, for instance, have a lot to do with what people think is happening. The psychological impact of the above report would be quite different if, for example, instead of saying that black medium income decreased one percentage point compared with white medium income in the previous year, the article had noted, what is statistically of equal validity, that between 1971 and 1972 the increase in white medium income was more than 200% greater than the increase in black medium income. (The figures reported are: black medium income, 1971: $6,440; black medium income, 1972: $6,864; white medium income, 1971: $10,672; white medium income, 1972: $11,549.)

lishment" on the basis of its "tactics." JDL's need for media coverage, in particular, had more than a little to do with this shift, and media was not lining up to cover JDL activities because they were an exemplification of "American moderation."

In considering the relation between "ethnicity" and public media and more generally the relation between absorption and media, it is worth quoting in full the concluding paragraphs of an article that appeared in *New York Magazine* about the Italian American Civil Rights League:

> Today, the views of some liberal politicians are changing, and New York's 1.6 million Italian-Americans are a key factor in that change. Similar ethnic revolts are taking place in other urban centers where the common needs of poor whites are breaking down barriers of ethnic xenophobia.
>
> "Nobody has done anything for the white working class since Social Security," Msgr. Geno Baroni, the director of the Center for Urban Ethnic Affairs in Washington, D. C. said. "Today, there is a budding national movement of white workers wonderfully parallel to where the blacks were a few years ago. My hunch is this one is going to move even faster."
>
> If Baroni is right, white ethnics will not only be the next glamor issue socially, but the basis for the kind of broad redistribution of economic power that every social revolutionary from Lenin to Bob Kennedy talked about. In New York, however, that working-class revolt will not have been sparked by the Central Labor Council, poli-sci radicals or the New York Review, but by a renegade rabbi [Kahane] and a Mafia boss [Columbo] (Pileggi 1971:36).

The posing of ethnicity as a glamour issue frames a key moment in the dialectic of absorption; each particular protest is encompassed—here through the medium of glamour—and thus the meaning of protest itself is effectively altered through this absorption. The passage speaks of "ethnic xenophobia" and "the blacks . . . a few years ago"—Italians, Jews, and any Other? Ethnicity is blatantly represented as a glamorous commodity, apparently available for the picking and the choosing. More startlingly, and more pointedly, the process of ethnic "revolt" is equated on a one-to-one basis with what almost appears to be presented as successfully accomplished "revolt" of blacks. The illusion of progress is substantiated through creation of an image of those protesting inequality as somehow enjoying a privileged status— that of glamor. But that status is presented as available to anyone; finally, if everyone is protesting and if everyone is thereby glamorous, the protests are not a major threat. This is the core of the issue. Indeed if everyone is protesting then no particular protest can become that much a threat. In the early 1960s, Marcuse wrote that political dissent through confrontation of those "outside the democratic process" offered a conceivable road toward "the beginning of the end of a period" (1964: 256-257). He notes, however, the potential for society to adjust or concede just enough "to the underdog" or to react through violence in order to maintain itself. The decade of the 1960s is witness to society's ability to respond with violence—but also, and perhaps more startlingly, to absorb social protest from within, to deflate confrontation through incorporating it, and to generalize the illusion of "popular sovereignty" to include even the "underdog."

Ethnicity and ethnic protest have become another self-sustaining system of meanings, created in the appropriation and appropriated in the creation. At first JDL created a new tactic by appropriating activism for a Jewish cause; but once that was done, the tactic soon became old-hat again; only through escalation could interest be preserved. Like fashion, the ethnic compendium of meanings seems to have no referents beyond itself, having been practicably dissociated from its own situation. Lefebvre *is* writing of fashion when he says of "essences" and of Ideas (like fashion) that they "appropriate every signification, every signifier, to signify themselves" (1968:164).[4] Ethnicity we are told has become fashionable, and through fashion one can indicate ethnicity. Finally, that media attention is given to JDL, the Italian American Civil Rights League (or hemlines, cuffed trousers, and eveningwear) becomes their equal "glamour."

The encouragement of (ethnic) internality is joined by the insistence on mutual comprehensibility; media in particular foster the belief that the Self is as knowable to the Other as to the Self. One might not wear the mask of "Jewishness," of "blackness," of "Italianness" (of "Otherness"?), but the choices can be displayed with glamour. The danger, however, is not the substitutable character of identities, per se, but rather the illusion without the reality, since, the consequence of ethnic substitutability is to engender and feed the belief in equality while concealing real inequalities. Difference has come to be demarcated through absolute similarity, and the terms through which rank is disputed are increasingly detached from anything but themselves. The imposition of racial and ethnic categorizations, with concomitant socio-economic limitations are now admitted and said to have prevented the full actualization of the egalitarian dream. But those same categorizations are employed to reinforce the dream's capacity to survive its repression. The terms of intended rectification, that is, are literally the same as those outlining the situation they are intended to alter. Specific needs and distinct programs of peoples with separate histories and in different situations can be evaporated in the panoply of presentation; each becomes a commodity, substitutable for each other. The implications of this discussion can be applied to the particular situation and program of the Jewish Defense League.

[4] In Lefebvre's words (1968:99), his "concern (with the insertion of fashion into everyday life) precedes or follows" analyses of Roland Barthes (1967).

Given JDL's open declaration that the responsibility of the American Jew was to Jews and, stated somewhat less directly, to Jews alone, JDL's construction of specific non-Jews has no necessary relation to those persons' and groups' own needs and motivations. JDLers saw themselves as dedicated to one broad end: "the survival of the Jewish people." Within the American context, that survival, despite warnings of a potential holocaust, was primarily socio-economic survival—as Jews. Conceptualizing groups of non-Jews was a double-ended process, for these Others were competitors in the struggle for "power" and defined what the Jew (or JDL) was not. Obviously individual JDLers joined the league with representations of Self and Other—with common-sensical personal notions of who and what they were in relation to notions about who and what Others were. When individuals joined JDL, their self-definitions were endowed with a concrete form and a wider status. We may now look at JDL's "ideological" stance toward relevant Others, a stance that was agreed upon by most JDLers, was in part presented or at least suggested in a variety of league publications, and was a permutation of American ideology, upholding the "value" of the autonomous individual who should ideally be offered the chance for "equal" political power ("democracy") and economic success.

JDLers designated "political extremists"—"radical left" and "radical right"—to be the greatest potential threat to the American Jew. The two extremes were differentiated, but the term "radical" carried more weight for most JDLers than did "left" or "right." JDL was here reflecting a familiar American assumption that communism and fascism are equally totalitarian (as opposed to "democratic"). League antagonism to the American radical left was said to be based on leftist support for Communist governments abroad and on the left's role in "frightening middle-Americans" so that they joined rightist movements. "Middle America," said Kahane during a speech at Columbia University, "does not find humor in Jerry Rubin sewing the flag to the bottom of his pants and sitting on it." In addition, JDLers saw the left as a political stronghold for "self-hating" Jews. The menace of the far right was clear: the recurrence of Hitlerite fascism. JDL demonstrated non-pacifically against the far right (e.g., the National Socialist White People's Party), and JDLers assaulted members of right-wing parties. For the most part, involvement with the left entailed demonstrations, counter-demonstrations and counter-counter-demonstrations. Physical contact of any sort, however, with either the right or left was not a daily JDL experience. When other groups were characterized as actually or potentially anti-Semitic, this threat was described as if it were the threat of "political extremism." In public presentation, stipulated anti-Semitism was explained as resulting from the failure of the "democratic process"; in the explanation, if not the specific aphorism, JDLers scarcely disagreed here with basic assumptions of a wider American ideology.

Groups with whom JDLers did have frequent, direct contact included the government, police, courts, undercover agents,[5] and non-Jews living in neighborhoods where JDLers resided. Non-Jews in New York City were broadly categorized by JDLers as WASPs, blacks, and white ethnics; among white ethnics, Italians were salient for JDLers and were characterized as the most sympathetic and least anti-Semitic of non-Jewish ethnic groups. With each of the other groups, JDL attempted to establish lines of commonality, often against a third or fourth group, but always to demarcate the Jew as distinct and ultimately separate from any of the Others.

JDL's most publicized "alliance" was that formed with the Italian American Civil Rights League (IACRL) led by

[5] Although undercover agents were not identifiable (if identified, they were no longer undercover), their constant presence was presumed by JDLers, who acknowledged that at any time those in the league office may have been observable by unsuspected government agents or through wiretaps and bugs. "Trust no one," said one active JDLer, "except yourself and the Reb."

Joseph A. Columbo, Sr. Although the actual tie became more sentimental than "practical" after the shooting of Columbo (June 1971), JDLers saw the alliance as representing mutually advantageous cooperation between ("grassroots") Jews and Italians. JDL maintained that such alliances offered the American Jew a necessary link with white ethnic America, a link not forged, according to JDL, by establishment Jewish groups, who, in the words of one leaguer "are more worried about going to parties with WASPs." JDLers used the link with IACRL as witness to their difference from establishment Jewry quite as much as to their similarity with white ethnic America. "That we joined with Columbo," reasoned JDLers, ". . . *that* sure shows people our *chutzpah*." To closely paraphrase Kahane:

> Most American Jews would rather not be Jewish. . . . It is the belief that they can join in the melting pot. There is no such thing as the melting pot. Only Jews melt. . . . The need of a people to have its own group is stronger than all the other internal longings. Columbo understood this. When he formed his group he said, "We are first." Well, we're not first—maybe twelfth—but if you can say, "first," people understand. . . . We understand Columbo and he understands us. The establishment Jew doesn't understand this intense yearning. He has made it. He's afraid of what the non-Jew will say. . . . He is constantly involved in playing a game of musical chairs. He goes to the annual Jewish-Christian banquet, and one year he gets a plaque from the Christians, and the next year he gives one to them. What he really wants is to be less Jewish minded, and he's slowly and subtly proceeding in that direction.

Officially, JDL described the link with IACRL as the joining of two groups, working for their mutual security and equality within the U. S.[6] Among JDLers, however, the

---

[6] Kahane and Colombo called the tie a joint effort to deal with government persecution of their respective groups. Colombo was known as having had underworld contacts. Kahane, along with several other

tie was more frequently taken to be an alliance against the "threat of black anti-Semitism" (black power) to "Jewish survival" (Jewish power), and was used as a model for inter-action in New York neighborhoods populated by Italians, Jews, blacks, and Puerto Ricans. JDLers describe "street fights" between Jews and blacks in which

> Italians joined on our side because we joined with Co-lumbo. . . . People say they're [IACRL] Mafia, but even if they are, we value survival more than respectability, and if Columbo says it's not good to be anti-Semitic, a lot of Italians will think twice. . . . We need allies and . . . Italians have a very good strong image.

Lines of alliance and antagonism between groups differed slightly from neighborhood to neighborhood. A social worker in one Brooklyn neighborhood where many JDL supporters lived explained that

> here Italians and Irish and other whites will combine against Jews, but they'll combine with Jews and Jews will combine with them against blacks or Puerto Ricans. Puerto Ricans here are against Jews and other whites and blacks, too. . . .Blacks—there aren't many in this neigh-borhood, so it's somewhat hypothetical—combine with Puerto Ricans against Jews and whites, but they're against Puerto Ricans also. . . .

Particularly in the league's first couple of years, the large majority of members joined JDL because, in the words of one JDLer, "they were really afraid of blacks, a lot of them . . . they live in the neighborhoods where there's crime . . . and also they're pissed at the concessions white liberals—and I mean WASPs and WASHes [White Anglo-Saxon Hebrews] —make to black militants . . . at the expense of the Jew."

JDLers, had been arraigned in court for conspiracy to violate federal gun control laws on the morning he and Colombo made their tie known.

The league denied a racist stance—a group claiming to exemplify "American moderation" could hardly do otherwise. "If you think," said one JDLer, speaking publicly, "because someone is black, he should have a greater license to beat you up, you're not only a fool but a racist." In a public effort to attest to such egalitarian sentiment, the league exchanged promises of "brotherhood" with a group called NEGRO (National Economic Growth and Reconstruction Organization), headed by Dr. Thomas Matthew.[7] JDLers also pointed to the selection of a black Jew for an "important leadership position" within the movement; concomitantly, however, they stressed among themselves that this person's identity as a Jew encompassed his being black. Activities which engaged JDL in its first year of existence were defense against crime, imputed almost exclusively to blacks, although blamed on a WASP city government and against the apparent emergence of black power, particularly in the city's public school system and universities. Commonly JDLers translated fear of crime into fear of blacks and vice versa, and then gave that fear "ideological" support; in the final translation, fear of blacks became the rational fear of political anti-Semitism. Instances of black anti-Semitism, verbalized especially in the course of the 1968 New York City school strike, were quoted in justifying "Jewish defense" intentions of the league. Indeed JDL's first action was occasioned when New York University hired John Hatchett to direct its Martin Luther King, Jr., Afro-American Student Center. Hatchett had authored an anti-Semitic article in *Forum*, the official publication of the Afro-American Teachers Association in 1967.[8] When a dozen or

[7] The association between JDL and NEGRO lapsed quickly, having had few consequences beyond the press notice it provided each. "We didn't have much to give them," said one JDL leader, "and they didn't have much to give us."

[8] Hatchett's article reads in part: "We are witnessing today in New York City a phenomenon that spells death for the minds and souls of our Black children. It is the systematic coming of age of the Jews who

so JDLers picketed before NYU that summer, JDL attained an early note in the *New York Times*. "Little did the paper or its readers suspect," writes Kahane in his *The Story of the Jewish Defense League*, "that within a brief period of time the new group would become the most well-known Jewish organization in the world" (1975:94).

In discussing anti-Semitism in America, particularly when speaking before public audiences, JDLers drew a distinction between de jure and de facto anti-Semitism, the first referring to irrational hatred of the Jew and the second to Jewish problems arising not specifically because the Jew is a Jew but because the Jew is there.[9] JDL upheld the assertion that, although de jure and de facto anti-Semitism may have stemmed from dissimilar causes, the Jew had to react similarly to both. JDL's justification for this often repeated belief varied from "a Jewish problem is a Jewish problem no matter who or what causes it and no matter who else may suffer along with the Jew" to "de facto anti-Semitism will lead eventually to de jure anti-Semitism if not stopped." The "American Jewish establishment," in the words of one JDLer, "does not understand this." He continued:

> Our point of view is, if a Jew is hurt, it's a de facto Jewish problem, whatever the reason. . . . What would have been the difference if Hitler had said he wasn't doing it to

dominate and control the educational bureaucracy of the New York Public School system and their power-starved imitators, the Black Anglo-Saxons. It is the avowed thesis of this paper that this coalition or collusion or whatever one chooses to call it, is one of the fundamental reasons why our Black children are being educationally castrated" (*Afro-American Teachers Forum*, November-December 1967).

9 This distinction is drawn from Vladimir Jabotinsky's differentiation between the "Antisemitism of men" and the "Antisemitism of things"; "the one is a subjective repulsion, strong enough and permanent enough to become anything from a hobby to a religion; the other is an objective state of things which tends to ostracize the Jew almost independently of whether his neighbors like or dislike him" (Jabotinsky 1942:53).

Jews but to non-Aryans. . . . Someone who doesn't understand this lacks understanding of *ahavat Yisroel.*

The league's "Movement Handbook" reads, "Reverse discrimination, quotas, changing Jewish neighborhoods, crime
against Jews, are all *de facto* Jewish problems when the Jew
is a victim" (p. 23). A particular target of JDL's programs
to hamper, if not eliminate de facto anti-Semitism was the
affirmative action program of the U. S. government. Affirmative action, a direct result of an executive order issued
during the administration of Lyndon Johnson, was aimed
against discrimination in public hiring, particularly discrimination against "minority groups" and women. Government contractors, including universities, were to demonstrate compliance with hiring guidelines or risk forfeiting
federal funding. JDLers viewed affirmative action as a guise
for new discrimination, against Jews particularly, whom
they said were "being asked to pay for the sins of John
Lindsay and Nelson Rockefeller's ancestors." The league
"Movement Handbook" reads:

> The imposition of a quota system to displace merit will
> hurt no other group as much as the Jews. We will have
> suffered twice. We remember the quota system of the past
> as an horrendous obstacle to obtaining higher education
> and jobs. . . . Indeed the great number of Jewish civil
> servants is due to past lack of opportunity to become
> professionals. . . .
> Quotas in schools will be followed by quotas in civil
> service and in industry and in opportunity in life. For a
> people who comprise 3% of the population, the thought
> is devastating (p. 23).

JDLers saw themselves, and other Jews who were not
wealthy, as being particularly vulnerable to the consequences of affirmative action programs, but believed that
"in the end all Jews will suffer from this." The league demonstrated publicly against affirmative action, and in one such

demonstration JDLers went to Shea Stadium where they demanded that the Mets, as a baseball team in a city with a large Jewish population, should be at least one-third Jewish. The JDL demonstrators had meant their protest to be humorous and were somewhat perturbed when the baseball team and the news media began to interpret the protest "seriously." Yet despite the league's vehement objections to affirmative action, the terms in which JDL condemned the program were similar to the terms in which others defended it.

In general, affirmative action is a key data source for the analysis of the egalitarian American ideology, since it is a government-administered program ostensibly admitting and working to correct inequalities within the "American system."[10] At this point I shall only touch the surface of such an analysis in suggesting that while affirmative action and other related programs are developed to correct inequalities, they simultaneously cause the absorption of protest by reenforcing the substitutability of ethnic categories. Affirmative action was established to eliminate discriminations resulting from "race, color, religion, sex or national origin" (Executive Order 11246 as amended by Executive Order 11375).[11] Universities, for instance, that receive federal funding are required to establish "guidelines" for hiring minority groups and women and to adhere to the guidelines within the time limits set.[12] JDLers objected especially to college

[10] Similarly, analysis of the premises and programs of the Office of Economic Opportunity in the late 1960s and early 1970s would be valuable in the effort to apprehend the way in which the government defined and dealt with socio-economic inequalities.

[11] The legal foundations of the affirmative active program include Title VII of the 1964 Civil Rights Act as amended by Equal Employment Opportunity Act 1972, and Executive Order 11246 (1965), amended by Executive Order 11375 (1967). This order was in turn amended during the Nixon administration by Executive Order 11478 (1969).

[12] Columbia University, for example, was informed by the Office of Civil Rights of HEW that unless guidelines were established and enacted the university risked losing contract awards. Columbia was made

and university questionnaires handed out to students and employees in order to determine the racial, religious, sexual, and ethnic composition of schools. "Merit," say JDLers, "and not race should be the basis for getting a job or into a school." Proponents of affirmative action would clearly agree and add that this exactly demarcates the need for the program.

A discussion among several JDLers about affirmative action and the selection of groups specifically included within universities' guidelines is indicative of JDLers' ambivalences about their own identification in comparison to what they called "third world groups." Several leaguers were perusing the list of ethnic and racial groups that had been included in a questionnaire handed out by Brooklyn College to its personnel in order to determine the composition of the staff

---

ineligible for new awards until the university showed it was making efforts to comply with Executive Order 11246. Guidelines were developed on the basis of "hiring pools." Several sources were employed to ascertain how the existent Columbia faculty, for instance, compared with the composition of the available "hiring pool," defined as "a group of people who share the same job-related characteristics and skills" (Columbia University Affirmative Action Program. Condensed Version. December 1972:3). Several data sources were employed including a "national 'census' of women doctorates" (ibid.). In addition the university estimated that 60% of its faculty had received graduate degrees from Columbia, Harvard, Berkeley, and Yale. The composition of persons holding advanced degrees from these schools was used as a basis for Columbia's guidelines. If the graduates of these four schools in a particular field were 10% women, then at least 10% of the faculty in the same field (department) at Columbia should be women. (Obviously this method for establishing guidelines ignores the basis according to which graduate-student bodies are selected.) It was possible to obtain "pool data" for women, the university asserted, but difficult to compile for minority groups. One estimate quoted "suggests that Blacks constitute less than 1% of the national pool of doctorates" (ibid.). The university concluded that for minority groups "there would seem to be no reliable standard for determining deficiencies except failure to exercise all reasonable efforts to recruit from among these groups" (ibid.).

(instructional, administrative, and custodial). The list contained the following categories, numbered respectively from one to eight: black; white; Puerto Rican; Spanish; Oriental; American Indian; Italian American; other. "How," asked one elderly JDLer, "did I get to be an other? . . . and all my life I've been poorer than half the people in those groups listed there." A second person added: "the problem is they [liberals] don't see us as a third world group so they're not afraid of us." After about a half hour of discussion, the JDLer who had first asked how he "got to be an other" concluded, "they're getting scared of us, but so what? We lose coming and going . . . we're only 3% of the population."

Yet black activist groups, particularly, served as conscious models for JDL's development. Comparisons between the league and militant black groups were made by friends and enemies of both and were taken up by JDLers themselves. Images of "Jewish panthers" provided a compelling referent in working out the meaning of "chaya," since JDLers' conceptual relations to "Black Panthers" involved opposition *and* emulation. "Black Panthers"—often used interchangeably by JDLers with "black power" or "black militants"—were deemed to have succeeded in doing for blacks what JDL hoped to do for Jews. A substantial part of that success, broadly framed as the attaining of power in a white gentile society, was explained to have been built on "black organization and discipline." JDLers, for instance, urged each other to undertake various tasks—from participating in actions to maintaining order at meetings to putting stamps on league correspondence—with the exhortation, "the Black Panthers are so successful because they do these kinds of things." "If," said Kahane in a public speech, "Shirley Chisolm can walk around saying black problems come first for blacks—Beautiful! Right on! Black problems *do* come first for blacks—then Jewish problems must come first for Jews." JDL expressly employed Jewish transformations of slogans and styles associated with black power (e.g., "Jew-

ish is beautiful" insignias). Young JDLers sought a naturalization of life-style, embodying Jewish parallels to "black is
beautiful." Many non-Orthodox JDL males wore yarmulkas
as a sign of Jewishness (rather than of Judaism). One JDL
woman in her early twenties explained that since joining
the league she stopped setting and straightening her hair;
"I used to straighten it because it seemed animal-like, but
now it's a question of Jewish identity not to . . . that happened to blacks when they got their movement." JDL
envisioned the black movement of the 1960s to be both a
cause *and* a model for the league's own struggle. Blacks
were thought to have "gained government concessions"
through militance, and JDL wanted to do the same, but
those very concessions were viewed as a "threat" to the Jew.
To paraphrase one JDL leader:

> The government, made up of WASPs, is willing to throw
> Jews to the dogs to save themselves. The Jew must make
> an intense militant effort just like the blacks did, or he'll
> be pushed out like in Europe in the 20s and 30s. Life will
> become impossible for Jews—politically, socially, and
> eventually physically. . . .

The ways in which JDLers ranked Jews in comparison
with groups of non-Jews are revealing in attempting to
understand JDLers' ambivalences about the Jewish establishment, blacks, and the league itself. Of thirty-nine JDLers
whom I asked to rank "different groups" in America, almost
all included only ethnic or racial groups in their responses.[13]
One person included the "government," one, "lower-classes"
and "upper-classes" and two, "extremist groups"; neither of
the two persons who mentioned "extremist groups" made
finer distinctions. Of the thirty-nine persons asked, the initial reaction of eleven was to place Jews first. Five of those
eleven followed Jews with, respectively, white Protestants,

[13] My request to these people left it up to them to decide what "ranking" meant.

white ethnic groups, blacks.[14] Of these five persons, two included Puerto Ricans, one ranking them before blacks and one after. Of the eleven who placed Jews first, two placed blacks second. Twenty-four people placed Jews in the lowest or second lowest rank.[15] In each case Jews were either followed by or preceded by blacks and/or Puerto Ricans and/or "third-world groups." No one offered subcategories within the category Jew.

The responses clearly clump into two contrasting sets. Almost one-third ranked Jews above other groups and almost two-thirds ranked Jews below. Although I claim no statistical validity for these results, they are startling enough to require an explanation. JDLers, it seems, employed two fundamentally different sets of assumptions in these rankings. When the thirty-nine people were questioned about the reasoning behind their rankings, all but two of those who ranked Jews first were imputing to Jews, and in several cases to each of the other groups as well, an essence, making for separate and impenetrable "ethnic" wholes. The persons who ranked Jews at the bottom were basing their responses on a consideration of the Jewish "position" in the sociopolitical world of "power" and "competition." Two of those who ranked Jews in an intermediate position, claimed also to be basing their responses on some combination of social, political, or economic power.[16]

[14] For the purposes of this presentation, I am listing as "white Protestant" the following responses: WASP, Protestants, Episcopalians, white *goyim* [non-Jews]. I am listing as "white ethnic groups" the following responses: Catholics, Italians, Irish, and Poles (only two persons of the thirty-nine mentioned, respectively, Irish and Poles; one person said "Catholics"). The few responses which do not refer to ethnic or racial groups are not included in the presentation.

[15] Three persons placed Jews in intermediate positions and one said, "Jews first, *goyim* second," adding that no further distinctions were possible.

[16] Several of the eleven people who ranked Jews first seemed to be employing both sorts of scales—Jews were ranked first on the basis of an "ethnic essence," and non-Jews were thereafter ranked according to considerations of "power."

In explaining these rankings, I shall start with those based on "power." It is perhaps somewhat surprising that the majority of people who claimed to be ranking "power" groups placed Jews at the powerless end of these orderings. Two sorts of beliefs seem to have been involved in that ordering, one stressing a future (or more accurately, atemporal) situation, and one a present situation. Several people who ranked Jews as least powerful based that assessment on forebodings about a Jewish "fate" in America. To quote an extreme example:

> . . . in this country there'll be a major fighting war within the next five years or ten years. It will start when a Hitler-type leader arises in the white Protestants. Italians will then see Protestants have the power, and they'll turn against blacks and Jews, or maybe they'll help Jews a little. Then blacks will see Italians and Protestants have the power and the Jews will be the enemy of all . . . that's why Jews are really powerless.[17]

Of the twenty-four persons who ranked Jews at the bottom, seven placed them below all other groups. Of these, six stressed the likelihood of "another holocaust" in explaining their rankings. Among the persons who placed Jews in the penultimate rank (followed by blacks and/or Puerto Ricans and/or "third-world groups") at least three-fourths made reference to a disastrous fate awaiting American Jews, but only two of these people placed greatest stress on that possibility. Conclusions about the relatively powerless position of Jews were supported by a wide variety of claims including, "a Jew couldn't ever become President"; "there are

17 Obviously such representations can be grounded in JDL's "official" warnings about the potential for a holocaust in the U. S. Furthermore there is a millenarian tradition within Judaism, positing the coming of *Moshiach* (the messiah) in the Hebrew year 6,000 (mid-twenty-third century in the Christian calendar). Some Hasidic rebbes have predicted that the process may be speeded up and that the coming of Moshiach will be preceded by great hardships.

hundreds of thousands of poor Jews right here [in New York]"; "now with quotas [a reference to affirmative action] Jews get jobs last of anyone." There was an almost total lack of reference to what in other contexts JDLers call the "establishment" or "made-it" Jews. These JDLers, it appears, were ranking Jews on the basis of a particular Jewish situation, the situation of the "poor, religious Jew" around which JDL had initially defined itself. The response of one JDLer, when I asked about how her rankings fit with the image of the rich and successful American Jew is suggestive. "The important thing," she said, "is the Jewish community and not individual Jews. There are rich Jews that assimilated. I mean, we can't forget them either. . . . Some of them could almost make you anti-Semitic though . . . they have no Jewish self-respect."

The particular situation of the JDL Jew comes to the fore but under the pretext that it is a universal Jewish situation. The individualistic ideal of socio-economic progress is commuted into the inauthenticity of that progress (a form of assimilation) unless all Jews benefit equally. Refusing to acknowledge (or wishing not to acknowledge) individual success as Jewish success has parallels to a "game," known in various permutations and outlined by Jacques Lacan (1966) in writing of a psychoanalytic *"temps pour comprendre"* (time for understanding) and *"moment de conclure"* (moment of conclusion).[18] The following is Wilden's description of Lacan's version of the game:

> [there are] three hypothetical prisoners of which the first to discover whether he is wearing a black or a white patch on his back has been offered his freedom by the prison governor. The prisoners are not allowed to communicate directly. The governor has shown them three white and two black patches and has then fixed a white patch on each man's back.

[18] Some implications of this "game" were brought home to me in dialogue with Richard Parmentier.

Lacan analyzes the intersubjective process in which each man has to put himself in the place of the others and to gauge the correctness of his deductions through their actions in time, from the *instant du regard* to the *moment de conclure*. The first moment of the *temps pour comprendre* is a wait (which tells each man that no one can see two black patches), followed by a decision by each that he is white ("if I were black, one of the others would have *already* concluded that he is white, because nobody has as yet started for the door"). Then they all set off towards the door and all hesitate in a retrospective moment of doubt. The fact they *all* stop sets them going again. This hesitation will only be repeated twice (in this hypothetically ideal case), before all three leave the prison cell together (Wilden 1968:105-106).[19]

[19] Lacan's "game" is hypothetical. JoAnn Magdoff has told me about a variant form of the "game" that was really played, with economic stakes attached. The game was used, in the following form, by an American company in selecting one of three candidates to fill an open position. The three candidates were shown *two* white patches and one black patch and told that one of these would be placed on each person's back. The first person to discover the color of the patch on his back was to be given the job. The *moment de conclure* was not interpersonal. The winner walked out of the room, declaring, correctly, that his patch was white, since *all* the candidates had had white patches placed on their backs.

In the "non-hypothetical world" the guards lie and the captives win by expecting fraudulence and acting accordingly. In the version of the game depicted by Lacan, the possibility of the guard's having lied is minimized. Only if all three prisoners had been given black patches could the guard have logically deceived them, but each knows that the Others wear white patches. Presumably, one of the prisoners could have been given a blue or orange or green patch, but that would seem to be another game rather than a transformation of this game since the Other prisoners would have seen this sign of not "playing" by the rules.

Neither the game hypothesized by Lacan nor that employed by the company has a logical solution outside the context of the game's being played. The prisoners in Lacan's game can solve the puzzle confronting them only through their ability to discern what the other players see— through an interpersonal process of comprehension.

Allusions from the "game" abound, and despite similarities to JDLers' construction of the situation of Jews, differences (as often, between the "made-up" and the "real") are greater than the parallels. Paramount among the differences is that the prisoners, when freed, have resolved their difficulty; it is a logical game, not embedded in a larger socio-cultural matrix; the terms of success are transparent in the set-up. On the way to solution, however, the prisoners are in the midst of paradox since in their halting steps to the door each relies on the Others for confirmation of correct judgment; but each must realize that just as this dependence on the Others occurs, so these Others are similarly dependent on oneself who, after all, does not know except insofar as the Others are trusted. Analogizing from this game to real people and groups is possible precisely because of the opacity of the individualistic Western "universe." In attempting to clarify one's place in relation to the social whole, the individual must rely on relative rank or status in comparison to another. But that Other, equally muddled, also relies on the first person or on some third Other.

JDLers who ranked Jews as relatively powerless, and when asked, explicitly excluded "successful" Jews from the relevant "community" being ranked, were implying that individuals who had "made-it" through assimilation were not part of the group, "Jews." As individuals they might still have been (almost surely were) seen as Jews, but they had separated themselves from the community in the eyes of JDLers. Their steps were no longer seen to be synchronized with the steps of the community. For purposes of socio-political comparison, poor Jews, oppressed Jews, and religious Jews (or, individuals who so identify by joining JDL) were *all* Jews.

This construction of the Jewish community has roots in the situation of Jews in pre-World-War-II Europe. In fact, over three-fourths of the thirty-nine people questioned either were born in Europe or were the children of immigrants. (This is a higher percentage of first or second generation Americans than is representative of JDL as a whole.) Within the *shtetl* (small town of Eastern Europe) the locus of valorization was the individual; each person was thought to be "naturally" different but not, ideally, better or worse. But before the gentile, the collective whole was one and alike, and was conceived as different from non-Jews. Mark Zborowski and Elizabeth Herzog (1969) in their ethnography of the shtetl write:

> A series of contrasts is set up in the mind of the shtetl child, who grows up to regard certain behavior as characteristic of Jews, and its opposite as characteristic of Gentiles. Among Jews he expects to find emphasis on intellect, a sense of moderation, cherishing of spiritual values, cultivation of rational, goal-directed activities, a "beautiful" family life. Among Gentiles he looks for the opposite of each item: emphasis on the body, excess, blind instinct, sexual license, and ruthless force. The first list is ticketed in his mind as Jewish, and the second as goyish (1969:152).

For about 150 years before World War II, assimilation became an increasing possibility, demanded or encouraged from outside (as in government decrees forcing shtetl children to attend secular schools) and from inside (as in the *Haskala* movement, which began the revival of the Hebrew language as a medium for secular, modern thinking). The notion of the "exceptional" Jew, however, is particularly pertinent to the present discussion. These Jews, especially well-educated and involved in secular non-Jewish society, were deemed "exceptional Jews" by Jews and non-Jews (and by themselves). Hannah Arendt writes that these assimilated nineteenth-century European Jews in their

> effort to distinguish themselves, created a Jewish type that is recognizable everywhere. Instead of being defined by nationality or religion, Jews were being transformed

into a social group whose members shared certain psychological attributes and reactions, the sum total of which
was supposed to constitute "Jewishness." In other words,
Judaism became a psychological quality and the Jewish
question became an involved personal problem for every
individual Jew (1958:66).

By excluding what was seen as (the American counterpart
to) the "assimilated" and "successful" Jew from the definition of the Jewish community, it was possible for JDLers to
construct the Jewish community as a coherent whole along
economic and socio-political, more than psychological, dimensions. This construction, however, depended upon a
model of society that itself assumed assimilation—but at
the group level. Jews were distinct, but at the expense of
being fully incorporated within the dominant society, defined in terms of "power"; that is, each group stands in
metaphoric relation to all other groups, which together are
absorbed in the larger, encompassing whole.

What JDLers meant by "power" (in the context of these
rankings) entails a notion of "class." In the words of one
JDLer:

> Those powerful, upper-class people, they don't have to
> tell the truth. . . . They all have money and are all upper-
> class. That's really where it's at. . . . They're not like us;
> they're not like the Reb, say. . . . The Reb tells the truth
> and he has no big power . . . we have no money. Guys
> like Rockefeller or Lindsay or ——— [the name of the
> wealthy president of a secular Jewish organization] don't
> have to tell the truth because they're upper-class.

There are two forms of power, vis-à-vis class, subsumed in
the premises behind the rankings. In the first place to be
upper-class (or "upper-middle class") was seen as power,
and in the second place to be able to control the upper-
classes to one's (individual or group) advantage was also

seen as power. Particularly those JDLers who ranked blacks or Puerto Ricans or "third-world groups" above Jews, in addition to stressing the possibility of another holocaust, explained that these groups could, in the words of one person, "get things from the government or white liberals, and Jews can't get that." The assumption of powerlessness was an appraisal of reality and something more: Most JDLers did feel beset with relative impotence in their everyday lives; yet to be defined as a powerless group was, ironically, posed as a route to power. Personal difficulty became comprehensible when explained as part of a group situation, for a group's demands for rectification become legitimate—or become, at any rate, equivalent to the demands of the Others.

The assumptions of people who ranked Jews first (with the exception of two people)[20] were not in opposition to the evaluative assumptions of people who ranked Jews at the bottom but were based in a different domain. (As will be shown below, the two sets of assumptions do interconnect.)

People who ranked Jews first did define the community according to a psychological quality but ostensibly a quality developed (for all Jews) within Jewish "history" and neither imposed by nor related to non-Jews. Six of the nine persons who ranked Jews first and explained that ranking on the basis of a quality stressed the importance of the Jewish "scholar," and the concept of the scholar does best sum up the essential identity referred to. This scholar-ness is a backward-looking quality, held to exist without particular regard for its contemporary manifestation in each Jew; it is almost a quality of birth (blood), a "natural" right, a priori present whether manifest or not. These respondents

[20] The two persons who did assert that Jews have a great deal of socio-economic power in the United States were the most marginal to JDL of the thirty-nine questioned. Both left JDL within a short while after joining and as a result of disagreement with league policy rather than, as was more generally the case, through declining interest not based on articulated differences of opinion.

tended to depict what is an almost Lamarckian view of evolution. To closely paraphrase one JDL leader:

> The only thing that's different about the Jews is the heritage that they carry. It's a people that sat studying for 2,000 years while other people were scratching themselves. Over the years, with inter-breeding, the group will excel in that which they do primarily.[21]

Being a scholar and the augmentation of scholarly qualities through practice (code for conduct) were seen as having become "natural" and definitive aspects of a Jewish heritage (blood). Blood and code for conduct were posed as mutually supportive and even equivalent, though not necessarily unalterably so. This Jewish predisposition could be negated in society, but that negation would presumably take centuries (2,000 years?) to complete. In light of the previous discussion about the synonymity of blood and code for conduct in the universe of caste hierarchy, it should be pointed out that that identity is based in transactions between caste (defined through purity and impurity) while the equivalence presumed by JDLers had, theoretically, nothing to do with Others (non-Jews). Furthermore, while out-casting is possible in India, the Jewish predisposition, once inherited, cannot be significantly depleted except through a very long period of time. The point is that, for JDLers, the identity posited between substance and code for conduct represents merely an assumed connection, not impugned by actual conduct in the world. Substance is only minimally altered by conduct or, rather, substance is in part the result of conduct, but the heritage carries more weight than present everyday action. This is in clear contrast to "ideological" representations of how to become a JDLer, where action is preeminent.

[21] This remark was made in a context other than that of explaining the rankings, but is being reproduced here because it is a particularly clear expression of a perspective held by many JDLers.

The contrasting modes of ranking Jews vis-à-vis other groups do not indicate general disagreement between the people who ranked Jews at the top and those who ranked Jews at the bottom. Both sets of people agreed that "if you look at it in that way" the alternative ranking was equally valid. A sense of Self as inferior was conjoined, by almost all, with a sense of Self as superior. In this presentation I have sorted out assumptions underlying the two modes of ranking on the basis of JDLers' explanations of their own specific rankings. In everyday thought and action the premises behind each type of ranking were intermingled and confused. One JDLer did discuss the relation between Jewish powerlessness in the socio-political word and Jewish superiority in abstract fact, and offered a model that provides clues for understanding the JDL "ideological" position in regard to and within American ideology.

With his hand, this person drew four imagined circles on a table. The circles were placed one under the other and decreased in size from the top to the bottom. The first circle he labeled WASPs, the second Italians (at one point he included other "white ethnic groups" along with Italians), the third blacks, and the fourth Jews. The decreasing size, he said, represented decreasing power and the top to bottom placement, an increasingly untenable "fate" within the "next ten years" in the U. S. He went on to say that each of the four groups could be "described" by a definitive quality:

> WASPs—they have the power. Real power, like government. . . . Italians have strength like the Mafia and the Italian [American] Civil Rights League. . . . That keeps them stable. . . . Blacks have common sense. If Jews had common sense they'd be a lot better off. . . . The trouble of the Jew comes because he has no common sense. But Jews have intelligence.

He continued, saying that although Jews have least power they are "superior" to the other groups, but "being superior doesn't do any good. . . . People are always against the Jews because they think Jews are superior."[22]

The inferior position of Jews with regard to power was explained as resulting from society's reactions to precisely that quality making the Jew superior. Additionally, Jewish powerlessness was seen as consequent to the lack of the other qualities (power, strength, common sense), but that is somewhat redundant, since these qualities themselves represent power. The superiority seen to balance *and* produce Jewish inferiority was surmised from an evaluation of the Jewish heritage; it is a superiority defined *in the group's own terms.*

The essentializing qualities assigned to the respective groups (from WASPs to Jews) become decreasingly tangible, decreasingly represented by social institutions—by events Out There. Blacks and Jews, but not WASPs and white ethnics, were essentialized through states of mind rather than social institutions. Or, put another way, blacks and Jews were defined as races in a universe of power. Yet the essence of the Jew, seen as least adequate to the world of power, was taken to be the superior essence. There was a general tension within JDL between the explicit struggle

[22] This person shifted several times during the discussion between asserting that Jews are superior and that gentiles view them that way. At one point he claimed that Jews are not really superior at all, but that non-Jews use that allegation as an "excuse" for "hating" Jews. The image of the intelligent Jew is one image of the Jew sustained by the dominant society, an image generally among the more positive Jewish stereotypes. Yet anti-Semitic doctrines have posed Jewish intelligence as cause for fearing, oppressing, or finally exterminating the Jew. One only has to recall the *Protocols of the Elders of Zion*, widely read and accepted on several continents, for a model in which Jewish intelligence becomes Jewish conspiracy becomes the evil Jew. The anti-Semite, writes Sartre, sees the Jew as "completely bad, completely a Jew. His virtues, if he has any, turn to vices by reason of the fact that they are his; work coming from his hands necessarily bears his stigma . . ." (1965:33-34). The JDLer quoted above shifted between condemning what he saw as a Jewish stereotype held by non-Jews and appropriating that stereotype as his own—as fact.

for power (survival) within a non-Jewish world and the point-blank condemnation of that power and that world. In seeking power within the U. S., the black was viewed as *the* Jewish competitor, since only Jews and blacks were characterized as heavily dependent on others' sources of power.

If the Jewish essence was held to be worth anything in attaining power, it is in the field and institutions of education. Those institutions were not, however, viewed as tangible correlates to the Jewish essence because they are not Jewish but WASP institutions, part of WASP power. Apparent gains in black power within educational institutions and public school systems were therefore seen to be a major threat to Jewish power and to the Jewish essence. "Education" is defined as the Jewish domain within the social universe, reaffirming the notion of the Jewish scholar (even in a non-Jewish world, that is, in secular educational institutions) and providing the Jew with an avenue to power in the U. S.—education, in general, and teaching, in particular. (In addition, these assumptions are supported by memories of the pre-World-War-II era when the existence of a civil service system in public school hiring enabled Jews to attain professional employment despite widespread anti-Semitism in hiring.)

Perceived threats to Jews working in the field of education were labeled de facto anti-Semitism by JDLers. Yet for JDLers de facto anti-Semitism in the area of education (as opposed to other phenomena called de facto anti-Semitism, such as crime in Jewish neighborhoods) had some of the earmarks of de jure anti-Semitism, since premonitions of discrimination in education entailed a sense of threat to Jewish essence as well as to Jewish power. (JDLers were here responding, I suggest, more similarly to what they call the Jewish establishment than anyone would probably have cared to admit.)

JDLers said that they worked for all Jews including establishment Jews, even though they disapproved of the establishment and its acceptance of assimilation in the diaspora. In fact, they envied that establishment while rejecting and criticizing it. JDLers said that they represented the Israeli perspective and life-style in galut. In fact, their identity came from within the American context, however much they stressed their place in a chain of Jewish heroes. They constructed a model of interaction in which they, and they alone, mediated between Jews and non-Jews. In fact, they felt the pressures of being Jewish and little of the benefits the American Jew was said to have achieved; and equally, they looked at their life situation and did not see how it differed from the hardships they heard the dominant society saying other groups suffered. They defended a self-identity of authentic Jewishness while feeling denied the advantages that America told them attended Jewish identity: they felt powerless; the Jew was said to have power. They were poor; the Jew was said to be rich. They drove taxis and trucks; they feared not finding work at all; the Jew was said to be educated and professional. And, in the end, they too believed the dominant stereotypes of the Jew—as they believed the dominant stereotypes of the black, the Italian, the WASP—the Other. And they did not fully understand why, but believed they were tied to the ghettos and deprived of the successes of the Jew as well as the compensations they thought the poor non-Jew was receiving. As Jews they yearned for the essence of the scholar. But in America the scholar was a success and they were not. As poor Jews and unassimilated Jews they wanted to be middle-class, but that was to be American.

Claiming they were both scholar and chaya, they were endlessly on the verge of believing they were really neither —for as often as not they, themselves, defined the two as mutually exclusive. By embedding a History of scholar-chayas (mythic Jewish heroes) within a more proximate "history" of suffering (the holocaust), they could sustain the illusions (and the double-binds) of defending a natural identity in a form that is its very opposite; of playing chaya to the scholars and scholar to the chayas and never being caught between the two. Yet that is where JDLers were. In proclaiming that they, like any Other, deserved the compensations they believed America was paying, they had to define the Jewish community to exclude the successful Jew. And to regain the inclusive Jewish community (the shared past and common future) they said they defended, they attributed to themselves (and to all Jews) a Jewish essence whose manifestation in the American context seemed to belong to the "Other" Jew.

CHAPTER VI

Parable of the Motionless Dance

"I am told," writes Sartre in concluding *Anti-Semite and Jew*, "that a Jewish league against anti-Semitism has just been reconstituted. I am delighted; that proves that the sense of authenticity is developing among the Jews" (1965: 151). Sartre proceeds to express doubt about the possibility of this league's succeeding insofar as Jews "hesitate to participate because of a sort of modesty" (1965:151). Yet when a Jewish league against anti-Semitism was established in New York twenty years after Sartre wrote *Anti-Semite and Jew*, its project was somewhat unlike that envisioned by him. Sartre's "authentic" Jews would sacrifice assimilation, but only so that their children might not be forced to do the same. JDL's "authentic" Jews would sacrifice their own separatism only so that *their* children could stand aside. When Sartre wrote *Anti-Semite and Jew*, in Europe in the wake of World War II, Jews were situated as a "race"—despised passionately for *being* Jews. And the anti-Semite's "idea of the Jew" had to do with almost everything but the Jews themselves (Sartre 1965:17); it is easier to understand the anti-Semite without the Jew than the Jew without the anti-Semite.

Yet the two poles of Jewish inauthenticity that Sartre postulates are quite in tune with JDL's construction of the inauthentic Jew—"anti-Semitism" on one side and "masochism" on the other. Sartre writes:

> . . . in anti-Semitism he [the inauthentic Jew] denies his race in order to be no more than a pure individual, a man without blemish in the midst of other men; in masochism, he repudiates his liberty as a man in order to escape the sin of being a Jew and in order to seek the repose and passivity of a thing (1965:109).

These two sorts of inauthentic Jews are clearly parallel to JDL's "Old Jews" of the diaspora: the "self-hating" Jew and the "weak," unreacting Jew. But at this point JDL and Sartre diverge, for what Sartre takes to be a cultural construction, JDL incorporates as natural fact: that the Jews are unlike the non-Jews, not only, not even primarily, in conduct but in their very essence. It is also the case that JDL is hardly alone in this belief, and indeed the anti-Semite would disagree least of all.

While JDL consistently postulated a Jewish internality, represented by the league and proffered to all Jews, the stress of (individualistic) self-identification has shifted several times since the league began. Until it became a nationalistic movement, the league increasingly defined itself as an activist ethnic group and as essentializing the "human condition" while being part of the larger American society. Through the natural ties of blood (and that conduct that is incorporated through time into blood and nature) JDL postulated a shared identity with all Jews, held to be (statistically) alike in their predisposition toward being scholars. This is an identification that seems not to need the Other. And so Kahane can write of the religious Jew (as quoted in chapter three), "The Jew who waits an extra hour or two because he is unable to find kosher food near his place of work . . . is a Jew who is strong, disciplined and the master of his 'I'" (1971:205). Yet JDL equally defines itself in opposition to the Other—the anti-Semite—and now it is this very same religious Jew ("strong, disciplined, and the master of his 'I'") who is the weak Jew, the "patsy," the Old Jew of the diaspora—in Sartre's word the "masochist." It is this Jew whose image JDL seeks to reverse and within whom JDLers attempt to instill the understanding, if not the mettle, of the chaya—of Abraham and Moses and Judah Maccabee. But the Old diaspora Jews bring, along with lack of response to domination, anti-Semitism, and annihilation, twenty centuries of traditional religion and Orthodoxy. Their encompassment within JDL's internality is both authentification (of JDL's Jewish "universalism") and the link of (essential) contiguity with an ancient History of heroism, the substantialization of the past.

Comparison with Historic heroes was the metaphor that empowered JDL and at once distilled that power.[1] That Moses was a Jewish hero, an "authentic" Jew, and a Historic liberator is hardly disputable. JDL was not, however, merely telling History; the claim was for the increasing synonymity of History and "history," and it was that JDL *is* Moses, for Moses and JDL together created the "reality" of Jewish heroes (and, in the end, Moses existed for JDLers because Kahane did rather than the other way around). JDL's concern was not actually with History but with "history"-still-being-made; intentional constitution of History provided a reference frame for the construction of "history." Jewish internality was authorized through condensation (metonymization of metaphor), but in that authorization the anti-Semite attained equal ontological "reality" with "Moses." Although this equivalent, though opposing, ontological construction justified the effort to amalgamate scholar and chaya, in consequence identification of Self became remarkably reliant on identification of Other. Ethnic internality remained conceivable through the shifting of levels, the appropriation of alternate metaphors of identity.

It is not History that appropriates internality, but history; not Ideology, but ideology. Metonymization of metaphor (establishing internality) inevitably defines another mode of illusion in a society based on "substitution," since enacting internality is simultaneously to give it away. Or rather, the Western individualistic "universe" is at base a "universe" of metaphor. When, as Lefebvre says it, "the significant absence of a general code" is ignored, dissent is imperceptibly swallowed up in the very process of its own articulation. When JDL, for instance, struggled to natural-

---

[1] The remainder of this section has been informed by Seitel (1972) and through dialogue with Steve Barnett, JoAnn Magdoff, and Richard Parmentier.

ize its internal metaphors (to create "history"), JDLers were unaware how small a place they did occupy in American culture (ideology). At first JDLers appropriated external metaphors to create "Jewish panthers" and thereby helped deflect another group's internality, and at the same time JDLers tried to tie down floating signifiers and to anchor them in Ideology. But the very availability of floating signifiers enables anything to be anything (Lefebvre 1971); JDLers could say they were a modern Moses, and news media, for instance, could report that they were "Jewish panthers" (thus they were Jewish panthers). Or, JDLers could say they were "Jewish panthers," and media could ignore the story altogether (thus they were nothing at all). A group's internal identity can be attenuated (or eliminated) through appropriation by the larger society, and the part Althusser assigns to condensation (structurally similar to the condensations creating ethnic internality)—"the 'identity' of opposites in a real unity" (Althusser 1969:211)—becomes increasingly impossible. Within the larger whole, ethnicity itself becomes another "substitution." Or, in other words, the power of internality is negated by the larger metaphor, for when condensations through which internal identity is created are endlessly displaced (and displacing), the salient consequence is absorption by the dominant society—finally, a motionless dance.

Bibliography: *Works Cited*

Althusser, Louis. 1969. *For Marx*. Ben Brewster, trans. New York: Vintage Books.

―――. 1971. *Lenin and Philosophy and Other Essays*. Ben Brewster, trans. London: New Left Books.

The American Jew Today. 1971. *Newsweek*. March 1:56-64.

Andelman, David A. 1971. JDL: Dangerous Campaign to Harass Russians. *New York Times*. January 17: Sec. 4, p. 1.

Arendt, Hannah. 1958. *The Origins of Totalitarianism*. New York: The World Publishing Company.

―――. 1969. *On Violence*. New York: Harcourt, Brace and World, Inc.

―――. 1970. Zionism Reconsidered. In Michael Selzer, ed., *Zionism Reconsidered: The Rejection of Jewish Normalcy*. New York: The Macmillan Company. pp. 213-249.

Barnett, Marguerite Ross and Steve Barnett. 1975. Peasants and Radical Change: The Ideas of a Militant South Indian Untouchable. *Annals of the New York Academy of Sciences* 220:385-410.

Barnett, Steve. 1973a. The Process of Withdrawal in a South Indian Caste. In Milton Singer, ed., *Entrepreneurship and the Modernization of Cultures in South Asia*. Durham: Duke University Press. pp. 179-204.

―――. 1973b. Urban is as Urban Does: Two Incidents on One Street in Madras City, South India. *Urban Anthropology* 2(2):129-160.

―――. n.d. Identity Choice and Caste Ideology in Contemporary South India. In Kenneth David, ed., *Changing Identities in South Asia*. The Hague: Mouton. In press.

Barthes, Roland. 1967. *Système de la Mode*. Paris: Editions du Seuil.

Barthes, Roland. 1972. *Mythologies*. Annette Lavers, trans. New York: Hill and Wang.

Bateson, Gregory. 1972. *Steps to an Ecology of Mind*. New York: Chandler Publishing Company.

Bienstock, Herbert. 1971. *Current Economic Developments: Implications for the Jewish Community in the Metropolitan New York Area*. New York: Federation Employment and Guidance Service.

Buber, Martin. 1948. *Tales of the Hasidim: the Later Masters*. Olga Marx, trans. New York: Schocken Books.

Cicourel, Aaron V. 1970. Basic and Normative Rules in the Negotiation of Status and Role. In Hans Peter Dreitzel, ed., *Recent Sociology* No. 2. New York: The Macmillan Company. pp. 4-45.

Columbia University Affirmative Action Program (Condensed 1972 Version). New York: Columbia University.

Della Femina, Jerry, with Charles Sopkin. 1970. *From Those Wonderful Folks Who Gave You Pearl Harbor*. New York: Simon and Schuster.

Douglas, Mary. 1966. *Purity and Danger: An Analysis of Concepts of Pollution and Taboo*. London: Routledge and Kegan Paul.

Dumont, Louis. 1965a. The Functional Equivalents of the Individual in Caste Society. *Contributions to Indian Sociology* 8:85-99.

———. 1965b. The Modern Conception of the Individual. *Contributions to Indian Sociology* 8:13-61.

———. 1966. A Fundamental Problem in the Sociology of Caste. *Contributions to Indian Sociology* 9:17-32.

———. 1970. *Homo Hierarchicus*. Mark Sainsbury, trans. Chicago: The University of Chicago Press.

Elkins, Michael. 1971. *Forged in Fury*. New York: Ballantine Books.

Epstein, Jason. 1968. The Real McCoy. *The New York Review of Books*. March 13:12 (5), 31ff.

Fernandez, James. 1972. Persuasions and Performances: Of the Beast in Everybody . . . and the Metaphors of Everyman. *Daedalus* 101 (1): 39-60.

Freud, Sigmund. 1965. *The Interpretation of Dreams*. James Strachey, trans. New York: Avon Books.

Geertz, Clifford. 1968. *Islam Observed: Religious Development in Morocco and Indonesia*. New Haven: Yale University Press.

Glazer, Nathan. 1972. *American Judaism*. Second edition. Chicago: The University of Chicago Press.

Glazer, Nathan and Daniel Patrick Moynihan. 1970. *Beyond the Melting Pot: the Negroes, Puerto Ricans, Jews, Italians and Irish of New York City*. Cambridge: MIT Press.

Goodman, Walter. 1970. Interview: Meir Kahane. *Playboy*. October 19: (10), 69ff.

Gordon, Milton. 1964. *Assimilation in American Life*. New York: Oxford University Press.

Goren, Arthur A. 1970. *New York Jews and the Quest for Community: The Kehillah Experiment 1908-72*. New York: Columbia University Press.

Hertzberg, Arthur. 1972. *The Zionist Idea*. New York: Atheneum.

Jabotinsky, Vladimir. 1942. *The War and the Jew*. New York: The Dial Press.

Jakobson, Roman and Morris Halle. 1971. Fundamentals of Language. *Janua Linguarum* Vol. I. The Hague: Mouton.

Jastrow, Marcus, compiler. 1903. *A Dictionary of the Targunim: the Talmud Babli Yerushalami, and the Midrashic Literature*. Vol. I. London: Luzac and Company.

Kahane, Meir, Joseph Churba and Michael King. 1967. *The Jewish Stake in Vietnam*. New York: Crossroads Publishing Company.

Kahane, Meir. 1971. *Never Again!* Los Angeles: Nash Publishing.

———. 1975. *The Story of the Jewish Defense League*. Radnor, Pennsylvania: Chilton Book Company.

Katz, Mordechai. n.d. *An Historic Challenge. U.S.A.*: Machleket HaTarbut. Netsivut Betar.

Kaufman, Michael T. 1971. The Complex Past of Meir Kahane. *New York Times*. January 24: 1ff.

Kemnitzer, David. n.d. *Notes Toward a Marxist Theory of Culture: Problematic and Dialectic.* Manuscript.

Lacan, Jacques. 1966. *Écrits.* Paris: Editions de Seuil.

———. 1968. *The Language of the Self.* Anthony Wilden, trans. Baltimore: The Johns Hopkins Press.

Laqueur, Walter. 1972. *A History of Zionism.* New York: Holt, Rinehart and Winston.

Lazere, Haskell L. 1970. Haganah U.S.A. *Dimensions* 4(3): 7-12.

Leach, Edmund. 1964. Anthropological Aspects of Language: Animal Categories and Verbal Abuse. In Eric H. Lenneberg, ed., *New Directions in the Study of Language.* Cambridge: MIT Press.

Lefebvre, Henri. 1968. *The Sociology of Marx.* Norbert Guterman, trans. New York: Vintage Books.

———. 1971. *Everyday Life in the Modern World.* Sacha Rabinovitch, trans. New York: Harper and Row, Publishers.

Levenson, Joseph R. 1968. *Confucian China and its Modern Fate: A Trilogy.* Berkeley: University of California Press.

Lévi-Strauss, Claude. 1966. *The Savage Mind.* Chicago: University of Chicago Press.

MacPherson, C. B. 1962. *The Political Theory of Possessive Individualism.* Oxford: The Clarendon Press.

Magdoff, JoAnn and Janet Dolgin. n.d. The Ethnic Medium. *The Yearbook of Symbolic Anthropology.* Vol. 2. In press.

Marcuse, Herbert. 1964. *One-Dimensional Man.* Boston: Beacon Press.

———. 1968. *Negations: Essays in Critical Theory.* Jeremy J. Shapiro, trans. Boston: Beacon Press.

———. 1972. *Studies in Critical Philosophy.* Joris de Bres, trans. Boston: Beacon Press.

Marx, Karl. 1967. *Capital.* Samuel Moore and Edward Aveling, trans. Vol. I. New York: International Publishers.

Mayer, Martin. 1969. *The Teachers Strike: NY 1968.* New York: Harper and Row, Publishers.

Memmi, Albert. 1962. *Portrait of a Jew.* Elizabeth Abbott, trans. New York: The Viking Press.

Ogden, C. K. 1932. *Opposition: A Linguistic and Psychological Analysis.* Bloomington: Indiana University Press.

Pileggi, Nicholas. 1971. Risorgimento: The Red, White and Greening. *New York Magazine.* June: 26-36.

Rubinstein, Annette T., ed. 1970. *Schools Against Children: The Case for Community Control.* New York: Monthly Review Press.

Sartre, Jean-Paul. 1963. *Search for a Method.* Hazel E. Barnes, trans. New York: Vintage Books.

———. 1965. *Anti-Semite and Jew.* George J. Becker, trans. New York: Schocken Books.

Saussure, Ferdinand de. 1960. *Course in General Linguistics.* London: Peter Owen Limited.

Schechtman, Joseph. 1961. *Fighter and Prophet: The Vladimir Jabotinsky Story.* New York: Thomas Yoseloff.

Schick, Marvin. 1967. The New Style of American Orthodox Jewry. *Jewish Life* 34(3): 29-36.

Schneider, David M. 1968. *American Kinship: A Cultural Account.* Englewood Cliffs, N. J.: Prentice-Hall, Inc.

———. 1969. Kinship, Nationality and Religion in American Culture: Toward a Definition of Kinship. In Robert F. Spencer, ed., *Forms of Symbolic Action.* American Ethnological Society. Seattle: University of Washington Press. pp. 116-125.

Seitel, Peter. 1972. *Proverbs and the Structure of Metaphor among the Haya of Tanzania.* Ph.D. Dissertation. University of Pennsylvania.

Selzer, Michael, ed. 1972. *"Kike!"* New York: The World Publishing Company.

Sharon, Lynn. 1972. Kahane's Cant. *Jerusalem Post.* October 17: 18.

Shibutani, Tamotsu and Kian M. Kwan. 1965. *Ethnic Stratification: A Comparative Analysis.* New York: The Macmillan Company.

Silverman, Martin. 1969. Maximize Your Options: A Study

in Values, Symbols, and Social Structure. In Robert F. Spencer, ed., *Forms of Symbolic Action*. American Ethnological Society. Seattle: University of Washington Press. pp. 97-115.

―――. n.d. Making Sense: A Study of a Banaban Meeting. In Michael Lieber, ed., *Exiles and Migrants in Oceania*. Honolulu: University of Hawaii Press. In press.

Suhl, Yuri, ed. 1967. *They Fought Back*. New York: Crown Publishers.

Sykes, Christopher. 1965. *Cross Roads to Israel: Palestine from Balfour to Bevin*. London: The New English Library Limited.

Tauber, Gilbert and Samuel Kaplan. 1968. *New York City Handbook*. Garden City: Doubleday and Company.

This is Betar. 1952. Berit Trumpeldor of Southern Africa.

U.S.A. v. Chaim Beiber et al. 71 CR 479 (Eastern District. N. Y., July 23, 1971).

U.S.A. v. Meir Kahane 71 CR 479 (Eastern District. N. Y., May 15, 1972).

Vilar, Pierre. 1973. Marxist History, a History in the Making: Towards a Dialogue with Althusser. *New Left Review* 80:65-106.

Wallace, Anthony F. C. 1956. Revitalization Movements. *American Anthropologist* 58:264-281.

Weber, Max. 1968. *On Charisma and Institution Building*. Chicago: The University of Chicago Press.

Weisbord, Robert G. and Arthur Stein. 1970. *Bittersweet Encounter: The Afro-American and the American Jew*. Westport, Connecticut: Negro Universities Press.

Wilden, Anthony. 1968. Lacan and the Discourse of the Other. In Jacques Lacan, *The Language of the Self*. Anthony Wilden, trans. Baltimore: The Johns Hopkins Press.

Zborowski, Mark and Elizabeth Herzog. 1969. *Life is with People: The Culture of the Shtetl*. New York: Schocken Books.

Ziegler, Mel. 1971. The Jewish Defense League and its Invisible Constituency. *New York Magazine*. April 19: 28-36.

Index

Library of Congress Cataloging in Publication Data

Dolgin, Janet L   1947-
   Jewish identity and the JDL.

   Based on the author's thesis, Princeton University,
1974.
   Bibliography: p.
   Includes index.
   1. Jewish Defense League.   2. Jews in the United
States. I. Title.
E184.J5D57   301.45'19'24073   76-3255
ISBN 0-691-09368-7